Mometrix
TEST PREPARATION

Series 26

Exam Secrets Study Guide

DEAR FUTURE EXAM SUCCESS STORY

First of all, **THANK YOU** for purchasing Mometrix study materials!

Second, congratulations! You are one of the few determined test-takers who are committed to doing whatever it takes to excel on your exam. **You have come to the right place.** We developed these study materials with one goal in mind: to deliver you the information you need in a format that's concise and easy to use.

In addition to optimizing your guide for the content of the test, we've outlined our recommended steps for breaking down the preparation process into small, attainable goals so you can make sure you stay on track.

We've also analyzed the entire test-taking process, identifying the most common pitfalls and showing how you can overcome them and be ready for any curveball the test throws you.

Standardized testing is one of the biggest obstacles on your road to success, which only increases the importance of doing well in the high-pressure, high-stakes environment of test day. Your results on this test could have a significant impact on your future, and this guide provides the information and practical advice to help you achieve your full potential on test day.

Your success is our success

We would love to hear from you! If you would like to share the story of your exam success or if you have any questions or comments in regard to our products, please contact us at **800-673-8175** or **support@mometrix.com**.

Thanks again for your business and we wish you continued success!

Sincerely,
The Mometrix Test Preparation Team

Need more help? Check out our flashcards at:
http://MometrixFlashcards.com/Series26

Written and edited by the Mometrix Exam Secrets Test Prep Team
Printed in the United States of America

TABLE OF CONTENTS

Introduction

Thank you for purchasing this resource! You have made the choice to prepare yourself for a test that could have a huge impact on your future, and this guide is designed to help you be fully ready for test day. Obviously, it's important to have a solid understanding of the test material, but you also need to be prepared for the unique environment and stressors of the test, so that you can perform to the best of your abilities.

For this purpose, the first section that appears in this guide is the **Secret Keys**. We've devoted countless hours to meticulously researching what works and what doesn't, and we've boiled down our findings to the five most impactful steps you can take to improve your performance on the test. We start at the beginning with study planning and move through the preparation process, all the way to the testing strategies that will help you get the most out of what you know when you're finally sitting in front of the test.

We recommend that you start preparing for your test as far in advance as possible. However, if you've bought this guide as a last-minute study resource and only have a few days before your test, we recommend that you skip over the first two Secret Keys since they address a long-term study plan.

If you struggle with **test anxiety**, we strongly encourage you to check out our recommendations for how you can overcome it. Test anxiety is a formidable foe, but it can be beaten, and we want to make sure you have the tools you need to defeat it.

Secret Key 1: Plan Big, Study Small

There's a lot riding on your performance. If you want to ace this test, you're going to need to keep your skills sharp and the material fresh in your mind. You need a plan that lets you review everything you need to know while still fitting in your schedule. We'll break this strategy down into three categories.

Information Organization

Start with the information you already have: the official test outline. From this, you can make a complete list of all the concepts you need to cover before the test. Organize these concepts into groups that can be studied together, and create a list of any related vocabulary you need to learn so you can brush up on any difficult terms. You'll want to keep this vocabulary list handy once you actually start studying since you may need to add to it along the way.

Time Management

Once you have your set of study concepts, decide how to spread them out over the time you have left before the test. Break your study plan into small, clear goals so you have a manageable task for each day and know exactly what you're doing. Then just focus on one small step at a time. When you manage your time this way, you don't need to spend hours at a time studying. Studying a small block of content for a short period each day helps you retain information better and avoid stressing over how much you have left to do. You can relax knowing that you have a plan to cover everything in time. In order for this strategy to be effective though, you have to start studying early and stick to your schedule. Avoid the exhaustion and futility that comes from last-minute cramming!

Study Environment

The environment you study in has a big impact on your learning. Studying in a coffee shop, while probably more enjoyable, is not likely to be as fruitful as studying in a quiet room. It's important to keep distractions to a minimum. You're only planning to study for a short block of time, so make the most of it. Don't pause to check your phone or get up to find a snack. It's also important to **avoid multitasking**. Research has consistently shown that multitasking will make your studying dramatically less effective. Your study area should also be comfortable and well-lit so you don't have the distraction of straining your eyes or sitting on an uncomfortable chair.

The time of day you study is also important. You want to be rested and alert. Don't wait until just before bedtime. Study when you'll be most likely to comprehend and remember. Even better, if you know what time of day your test will be, set that time aside for study. That way your brain will be used to working on that subject at that specific time and you'll have a better chance of recalling information.

Finally, it can be helpful to team up with others who are studying for the same test. Your actual studying should be done in as isolated an environment as possible, but the work of organizing the information and setting up the study plan can be divided up. In between study sessions, you can discuss with your teammates the concepts that you're all studying and quiz each other on the details. Just be sure that your teammates are as serious about the test as you are. If you find that your study time is being replaced with social time, you might need to find a new team.

Secret Key 2: Make Your Studying Count

You're devoting a lot of time and effort to preparing for this test, so you want to be absolutely certain it will pay off. This means doing more than just reading the content and hoping you can remember it on test day. It's important to make every minute of study count. There are two main areas you can focus on to make your studying count.

Retention

It doesn't matter how much time you study if you can't remember the material. You need to make sure you are retaining the concepts. To check your retention of the information you're learning, try recalling it at later times with minimal prompting. Try carrying around flashcards and glance at one or two from time to time or ask a friend who's also studying for the test to quiz you.

To enhance your retention, look for ways to put the information into practice so that you can apply it rather than simply recalling it. If you're using the information in practical ways, it will be much easier to remember. Similarly, it helps to solidify a concept in your mind if you're not only reading it to yourself but also explaining it to someone else. Ask a friend to let you teach them about a concept you're a little shaky on (or speak aloud to an imaginary audience if necessary). As you try to summarize, define, give examples, and answer your friend's questions, you'll understand the concepts better and they will stay with you longer. Finally, step back for a big picture view and ask yourself how each piece of information fits with the whole subject. When you link the different concepts together and see them working together as a whole, it's easier to remember the individual components.

Finally, practice showing your work on any multi-step problems, even if you're just studying. Writing out each step you take to solve a problem will help solidify the process in your mind, and you'll be more likely to remember it during the test.

Modality

Modality simply refers to the means or method by which you study. Choosing a study modality that fits your own individual learning style is crucial. No two people learn best in exactly the same way, so it's important to know your strengths and use them to your advantage.

For example, if you learn best by visualization, focus on visualizing a concept in your mind and draw an image or a diagram. Try color-coding your notes, illustrating them, or creating symbols that will trigger your mind to recall a learned concept. If you learn best by hearing or discussing information, find a study partner who learns the same way or read aloud to yourself. Think about how to put the information in your own words. Imagine that you are giving a lecture on the topic and record yourself so you can listen to it later.

For any learning style, flashcards can be helpful. Organize the information so you can take advantage of spare moments to review. Underline key words or phrases. Use different colors for different categories. Mnemonic devices (such as creating a short list in which every item starts with the same letter) can also help with retention. Find what works best for you and use it to store the information in your mind most effectively and easily.

Secret Key 3: Practice the Right Way

Your success on test day depends not only on how many hours you put into preparing, but also on whether you prepared the right way. It's good to check along the way to see if your studying is paying off. One of the most effective ways to do this is by taking practice tests to evaluate your progress. Practice tests are useful because they show exactly where you need to improve. Every time you take a practice test, pay special attention to these three groups of questions:

- The questions you got wrong
- The questions you had to guess on, even if you guessed right
- The questions you found difficult or slow to work through

This will show you exactly what your weak areas are, and where you need to devote more study time. Ask yourself why each of these questions gave you trouble. Was it because you didn't understand the material? Was it because you didn't remember the vocabulary? Do you need more repetitions on this type of question to build speed and confidence? Dig into those questions and figure out how you can strengthen your weak areas as you go back to review the material.

Additionally, many practice tests have a section explaining the answer choices. It can be tempting to read the explanation and think that you now have a good understanding of the concept. However, an explanation likely only covers part of the question's broader context. Even if the explanation makes perfect sense, **go back and investigate** every concept related to the question until you're positive you have a thorough understanding.

As you go along, keep in mind that the practice test is just that: practice. Memorizing these questions and answers will not be very helpful on the actual test because it is unlikely to have any of the same exact questions. If you only know the right answers to the sample questions, you won't be prepared for the real thing. **Study the concepts** until you understand them fully, and then you'll be able to answer any question that shows up on the test.

It's important to wait on the practice tests until you're ready. If you take a test on your first day of study, you may be overwhelmed by the amount of material covered and how much you need to learn. Work up to it gradually.

On test day, you'll need to be prepared for answering questions, managing your time, and using the test-taking strategies you've learned. It's a lot to balance, like a mental marathon that will have a big impact on your future. Like training for a marathon, you'll need to start slowly and work your way up. When test day arrives, you'll be ready.

Start with the strategies you've read in the first two Secret Keys—plan your course and study in the way that works best for you. If you have time, consider using multiple study resources to get different approaches to the same concepts. It can be helpful to see difficult concepts from more than one angle. Then find a good source for practice tests. Many times, the test website will suggest potential study resources or provide sample tests.

Practice Test Strategy

If you're able to find at least three practice tests, we recommend this strategy:

Untimed and Open-Book Practice

Take the first test with no time constraints and with your notes and study guide handy. Take your time and focus on applying the strategies you've learned.

Timed and Open-Book Practice

Take the second practice test open-book as well, but set a timer and practice pacing yourself to finish in time.

Timed and Closed-Book Practice

Take any other practice tests as if it were test day. Set a timer and put away your study materials. Sit at a table or desk in a quiet room, imagine yourself at the testing center, and answer questions as quickly and accurately as possible.

Keep repeating timed and closed-book tests on a regular basis until you run out of practice tests or it's time for the actual test. Your mind will be ready for the schedule and stress of test day, and you'll be able to focus on recalling the material you've learned.

Secret Key 4: Pace Yourself

Once you're fully prepared for the material on the test, your biggest challenge on test day will be managing your time. Just knowing that the clock is ticking can make you panic even if you have plenty of time left. Work on pacing yourself so you can build confidence against the time constraints of the exam. Pacing is a difficult skill to master, especially in a high-pressure environment, so **practice is vital**.

Set time expectations for your pace based on how much time is available. For example, if a section has 60 questions and the time limit is 30 minutes, you know you have to average 30 seconds or less per question in order to answer them all. Although 30 seconds is the hard limit, set 25 seconds per question as your goal, so you reserve extra time to spend on harder questions. When you budget extra time for the harder questions, you no longer have any reason to stress when those questions take longer to answer.

Don't let this time expectation distract you from working through the test at a calm, steady pace, but keep it in mind so you don't spend too much time on any one question. Recognize that taking extra time on one question you don't understand may keep you from answering two that you do understand later in the test. If your time limit for a question is up and you're still not sure of the answer, mark it and move on, and come back to it later if the time and the test format allow. If the testing format doesn't allow you to return to earlier questions, just make an educated guess; then put it out of your mind and move on.

On the easier questions, be careful not to rush. It may seem wise to hurry through them so you have more time for the challenging ones, but it's not worth missing one if you know the concept and just didn't take the time to read the question fully. Work efficiently but make sure you understand the question and have looked at all of the answer choices, since more than one may seem right at first.

Even if you're paying attention to the time, you may find yourself a little behind at some point. You should speed up to get back on track, but do so wisely. Don't panic; just take a few seconds less on each question until you're caught up. Don't guess without thinking, but do look through the answer choices and eliminate any you know are wrong. If you can get down to two choices, it is often worthwhile to guess from those. Once you've chosen an answer, move on and don't dwell on any that you skipped or had to hurry through. If a question was taking too long, chances are it was one of the harder ones, so you weren't as likely to get it right anyway.

On the other hand, if you find yourself getting ahead of schedule, it may be beneficial to slow down a little. The more quickly you work, the more likely you are to make a careless mistake that will affect your score. You've budgeted time for each question, so don't be afraid to spend that time. Practice an efficient but careful pace to get the most out of the time you have.

Secret Key 5: Have a Plan for Guessing

When you're taking the test, you may find yourself stuck on a question. Some of the answer choices seem better than others, but you don't see the one answer choice that is obviously correct. What do you do?

The scenario described above is very common, yet most test takers have not effectively prepared for it. Developing and practicing a plan for guessing may be one of the single most effective uses of your time as you get ready for the exam.

In developing your plan for guessing, there are three questions to address:

- When should you start the guessing process?
- How should you narrow down the choices?
- Which answer should you choose?

When to Start the Guessing Process

Unless your plan for guessing is to select C every time (which, despite its merits, is not what we recommend), you need to leave yourself enough time to apply your answer elimination strategies. Since you have a limited amount of time for each question, that means that if you're going to give yourself the best shot at guessing correctly, you have to decide quickly whether or not you will guess.

Of course, the best-case scenario is that you don't have to guess at all, so first, see if you can answer the question based on your knowledge of the subject and basic reasoning skills. Focus on the key words in the question and try to jog your memory of related topics. Give yourself a chance to bring the knowledge to mind, but once you realize that you don't have (or you can't access) the knowledge you need to answer the question, it's time to start the guessing process.

It's almost always better to start the guessing process too early than too late. It only takes a few seconds to remember something and answer the question from knowledge. Carefully eliminating wrong answer choices takes longer. Plus, going through the process of eliminating answer choices can actually help jog your memory.

Summary: Start the guessing process as soon as you decide that you can't answer the question based on your knowledge.

How to Narrow Down the Choices

The next chapter in this book (**Test-Taking Strategies**) includes a wide range of strategies for how to approach questions and how to look for answer choices to eliminate. You will definitely want to read those carefully, practice them, and figure out which ones work best for you. Here though, we're going to address a mindset rather than a particular strategy.

Your odds of guessing an answer correctly depend on how many options you are choosing from.

Number of options left	5	4	3	2	1
Odds of guessing correctly	20%	25%	33%	50%	100%

You can see from this chart just how valuable it is to be able to eliminate incorrect answers and make an educated guess, but there are two things that many test takers do that cause them to miss out on the benefits of guessing:

- Accidentally eliminating the correct answer
- Selecting an answer based on an impression

We'll look at the first one here, and the second one in the next section.

To avoid accidentally eliminating the correct answer, we recommend a thought exercise called **the $5 challenge**. In this challenge, you only eliminate an answer choice from contention if you are willing to bet $5 on it being wrong. Why $5? Five dollars is a small but not insignificant amount of money. It's an amount you could afford to lose but wouldn't want to throw away. And while losing $5 once might not hurt too much, doing it twenty times will set you back $100. In the same way, each small decision you make—eliminating a choice here, guessing on a question there—won't by itself impact your score very much, but when you put them all together, they can make a big difference. By holding each answer choice elimination decision to a higher standard, you can reduce the risk of accidentally eliminating the correct answer.

The $5 challenge can also be applied in a positive sense: If you are willing to bet $5 that an answer choice *is* correct, go ahead and mark it as correct.

Summary: Only eliminate an answer choice if you are willing to bet $5 that it is wrong.

Which Answer to Choose

You're taking the test. You've run into a hard question and decided you'll have to guess. You've eliminated all the answer choices you're willing to bet $5 on. Now you have to pick an answer. Why do we even need to talk about this? Why can't you just pick whichever one you feel like when the time comes?

The answer to these questions is that if you don't come into the test with a plan, you'll rely on your impression to select an answer choice, and if you do that, you risk falling into a trap. The test writers know that everyone who takes their test will be guessing on some of the questions, so they intentionally write wrong answer choices to seem plausible. You still have to pick an answer though, and if the wrong answer choices are designed to look right, how can you ever be sure that you're not falling for their trap? The best solution we've found to this dilemma is to take the decision out of your hands entirely. Here is the process we recommend:

Once you've eliminated any choices that you are confident (willing to bet $5) are wrong, select the first remaining choice as your answer.

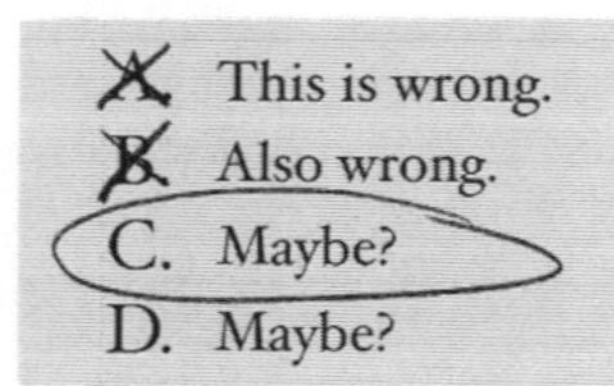

Whether you choose to select the first remaining choice, the second, or the last, the important thing is that you use some preselected standard. Using this approach guarantees that you will not be enticed into selecting an answer choice that looks right, because you are not basing your decision on how the answer choices look.

This is not meant to make you question your knowledge. Instead, it is to help you recognize the difference between your knowledge and your impressions. There's a huge difference between thinking an answer is right because of what you know, and thinking an answer is right because it looks or sounds like it should be right.

Summary: To ensure that your selection is appropriately random, make a predetermined selection from among all answer choices you have not eliminated.

Test-Taking Strategies

This section contains a list of test-taking strategies that you may find helpful as you work through the test. By taking what you know and applying logical thought, you can maximize your chances of answering any question correctly!

It is very important to realize that every question is different and every person is different: no single strategy will work on every question, and no single strategy will work for every person. That's why we've included all of them here, so you can try them out and determine which ones work best for different types of questions and which ones work best for you.

Question Strategies

☑ Read Carefully

Read the question and the answer choices carefully. Don't miss the question because you misread the terms. You have plenty of time to read each question thoroughly and make sure you understand what is being asked. Yet a happy medium must be attained, so don't waste too much time. You must read carefully and efficiently.

☑ Contextual Clues

Look for contextual clues. If the question includes a word you are not familiar with, look at the immediate context for some indication of what the word might mean. Contextual clues can often give you all the information you need to decipher the meaning of an unfamiliar word. Even if you can't determine the meaning, you may be able to narrow down the possibilities enough to make a solid guess at the answer to the question.

☑ Prefixes

If you're having trouble with a word in the question or answer choices, try dissecting it. Take advantage of every clue that the word might include. Prefixes can be a huge help. Usually, they allow you to determine a basic meaning. *Pre-* means before, *post-* means after, *pro-* is positive, *de-* is negative. From prefixes, you can get an idea of the general meaning of the word and try to put it into context.

☑ Hedge Words

Watch out for critical hedge words, such as *likely, may, can, often, almost, mostly, usually, generally, rarely,* and *sometimes.* Question writers insert these hedge phrases to cover every possibility. Often an answer choice will be wrong simply because it leaves no room for exception. Be on guard for answer choices that have definitive words such as *exactly* and *always.*

⊘ Switchback Words

Stay alert for *switchbacks*. These are the words and phrases frequently used to alert you to shifts in thought. The most common switchback words are *but*, *although*, and *however*. Others include *nevertheless*, *on the other hand*, *even though*, *while*, *in spite of*, *despite*, and *regardless of*. Switchback words are important to catch because they can change the direction of the question or an answer choice.

⊘ Face Value

When in doubt, use common sense. Accept the situation in the problem at face value. Don't read too much into it. These problems will not require you to make wild assumptions. If you have to go beyond creativity and warp time or space in order to have an answer choice fit the question, then you should move on and consider the other answer choices. These are normal problems rooted in reality. The applicable relationship or explanation may not be readily apparent, but it is there for you to figure out. Use your common sense to interpret anything that isn't clear.

Answer Choice Strategies

⊘ Answer Selection

The most thorough way to pick an answer choice is to identify and eliminate wrong answers until only one is left, then confirm it is the correct answer. Sometimes an answer choice may immediately seem right, but be careful. The test writers will usually put more than one reasonable answer choice on each question, so take a second to read all of them and make sure that the other choices are not equally obvious. As long as you have time left, it is better to read every answer choice than to pick the first one that looks right without checking the others.

⊘ Answer Choice Families

An answer choice family consists of two (in rare cases, three) answer choices that are very similar in construction and cannot all be true at the same time. If you see two answer choices that are direct opposites or parallels, one of them is usually the correct answer. For instance, if one answer choice says that quantity x increases and another either says that quantity x decreases (opposite) or says that quantity y increases (parallel), then those answer choices would fall into the same family. An answer choice that doesn't match the construction of the answer choice family is more likely to be incorrect. Most questions will not have answer choice families, but when they do appear, you should be prepared to recognize them.

⊘ Eliminate Answers

Eliminate answer choices as soon as you realize they are wrong, but make sure you consider all possibilities. If you are eliminating answer choices and realize that the last one you are left with is also wrong, don't panic. Start over and consider each choice again. There may be something you missed the first time that you will realize on the second pass.

☑ Avoid Fact Traps

Don't be distracted by an answer choice that is factually true but doesn't answer the question. You are looking for the choice that answers the question. Stay focused on what the question is asking for so you don't accidentally pick an answer that is true but incorrect. Always go back to the question and make sure the answer choice you've selected actually answers the question and is not merely a true statement.

☑ Extreme Statements

In general, you should avoid answers that put forth extreme actions as standard practice or proclaim controversial ideas as established fact. An answer choice that states the "process should be used in certain situations, if..." is much more likely to be correct than one that states the "process should be discontinued completely." The first is a calm rational statement and doesn't even make a definitive, uncompromising stance, using a hedge word *if* to provide wiggle room, whereas the second choice is far more extreme.

☑ Benchmark

As you read through the answer choices and you come across one that seems to answer the question well, mentally select that answer choice. This is not your final answer, but it's the one that will help you evaluate the other answer choices. The one that you selected is your benchmark or standard for judging each of the other answer choices. Every other answer choice must be compared to your benchmark. That choice is correct until proven otherwise by another answer choice beating it. If you find a better answer, then that one becomes your new benchmark. Once you've decided that no other choice answers the question as well as your benchmark, you have your final answer.

☑ Predict the Answer

Before you even start looking at the answer choices, it is often best to try to predict the answer. When you come up with the answer on your own, it is easier to avoid distractions and traps because you will know exactly what to look for. The right answer choice is unlikely to be word-for-word what you came up with, but it should be a close match. Even if you are confident that you have the right answer, you should still take the time to read each option before moving on.

General Strategies

☑ Tough Questions

If you are stumped on a problem or it appears too hard or too difficult, don't waste time. Move on! Remember though, if you can quickly check for obviously incorrect answer choices, your chances of guessing correctly are greatly improved. Before you completely give up, at least try to knock out a couple of possible answers. Eliminate what you can and then guess at the remaining answer choices before moving on.

⊘ Check Your Work

Since you will probably not know every term listed and the answer to every question, it is important that you get credit for the ones that you do know. Don't miss any questions through careless mistakes. If at all possible, try to take a second to look back over your answer selection and make sure you've selected the correct answer choice and haven't made a costly careless mistake (such as marking an answer choice that you didn't mean to mark). This quick double check should more than pay for itself in caught mistakes for the time it costs.

⊘ Pace Yourself

It's easy to be overwhelmed when you're looking at a page full of questions; your mind is confused and full of random thoughts, and the clock is ticking down faster than you would like. Calm down and maintain the pace that you have set for yourself. Especially as you get down to the last few minutes of the test, don't let the small numbers on the clock make you panic. As long as you are on track by monitoring your pace, you are guaranteed to have time for each question.

⊘ Don't Rush

It is very easy to make errors when you are in a hurry. Maintaining a fast pace in answering questions is pointless if it makes you miss questions that you would have gotten right otherwise. Test writers like to include distracting information and wrong answers that seem right. Taking a little extra time to avoid careless mistakes can make all the difference in your test score. Find a pace that allows you to be confident in the answers that you select.

⊘ Keep Moving

Panicking will not help you pass the test, so do your best to stay calm and keep moving. Taking deep breaths and going through the answer elimination steps you practiced can help to break through a stress barrier and keep your pace.

Final Notes

The combination of a solid foundation of content knowledge and the confidence that comes from practicing your plan for applying that knowledge is the key to maximizing your performance on test day. As your foundation of content knowledge is built up and strengthened, you'll find that the strategies included in this chapter become more and more effective in helping you quickly sift through the distractions and traps of the test to isolate the correct answer.

Now that you're preparing to move forward into the test content chapters of this book, be sure to keep your goal in mind. As you read, think about how you will be able to apply this information on the test. If you've already seen sample questions for the test and you have an idea of the question format and style, try to come up with questions of your own that you can answer based on what you're reading. This will give you valuable practice applying your knowledge in the same ways you can expect to on test day.

Good luck and good studying!

Personnel Management Activities and Registration of the Broker-Dealer

Hiring and Qualification

Form U4

Form U4 (Uniform Application for Securities Industry Registration or Transfer) is used by broker-dealers to register associated persons with the proper self-regulatory organizations and jurisdictions. The form must be completed by all representatives of broker-dealers, investment advisers, and issuers of securities. Additionally, associated persons must complete a new Form U4 upon beginning work at a new broker-dealer, investment adviser, or issuer of securities. In addition to filing Form U4 upon commencing employment as an associated person, any material changes must also be disclosed by submitting an updated U4 in a timely manner.

Form U4 (Uniform Application for Securities Industry Registration or Transfer) requires the disclosure of a significant amount of personal, professional, and criminal information. Personal information that registrants must disclose includes general information such as name (including any name changes), height, weight, hair color, eye color, gender, birthplace, Social Security number, employment date with the current member firm, and five years of residential history. The professional information that must be disclosed includes any professional designations, 10 years of employment history, any outside business activities, and registration with unaffiliated firms. Finally, Form U4 also requires the disclosure of any criminal history or regulatory action or complaints brought against the person.

Form U5

Form U5 (Uniform Termination Notice for Securities Industry Registration) is used by broker-dealers, investment advisers, or issuers of securities to terminate the registration of associated persons with the proper self-regulatory organizations and jurisdictions. Form U5 is only used in the case of a full termination. Upon a partial termination of only certain registrations or jurisdictions, the updates should be made using Form U4 (Uniform Application for Securities Industry Regulation or Transfer). If additional details relevant to Form U5 come to light after the initial filing of the form by the member firm, that member firm is obligated to electronically submit an amendment to Section 7 of Form U5.

Form U5 (Uniform Termination Notice for Securities Industry Registration) requires the disclosure of a significant amount of personal, registration, and termination information, as well as certain disclosures. Personal information that registrants must disclose includes general information such as name, Social Security data, general member firm identification information, and current residential address. The registration information that must be disclosed includes the nature of the termination (full or partial), the reason for termination, and the date of termination. Finally, the disclosure information requires the firm to disclose any investigations, internal reviews, criminal activities, or customer complaints and arbitration. Any affirmative disclosures within this section require the completion of an additional form (Internal Review Reporting Page) to provide further information.

Information Housed in the FINRA Central Registration Depository (CRD)

FINRA's Central Registration Depository (CRD) is the central licensing and registration system for the US securities industry and its regulators. This includes the registrations for broker-dealers, investment advisors, and issuers of securities, as well as the qualification, employment, and disclosures for all registered persons associated with FINRA members. More specifically, this means that the CRD houses all of the registrant's disciplinary history that is disclosed on that registrant's Form U4, including criminal history (felonies and investment-related misdemeanors), regulatory sanctions by the US Securities and Exchange Commission or Commodity Futures Trading Commission, sanctions by any other federal regulatory agency or foreign financial regulatory authority, and sanctions by a self-regulatory organization. In addition, the CRD houses information related to a registrant's history of investment-related civil judicial findings, customer complaints, arbitration findings, terminations for cause related to fraud or violation of laws, and personal bankruptcy proceedings.

FINRA's Central Registration Depository (CRD) is the central licensing and registration system for the US securities industry and its regulators. This includes the registrations for broker-dealers, investment advisors, and issuers of securities, as well as the qualification, employment, and disclosures for all registered persons associated with FINRA members. More specifically, this means that the CRD houses all of the information provided on the registrant's Form U4 with respect to current and past professional activities. This includes all employment history for the prior 10 years, including the employer's name, dates of employment, positions held, city, state, and country, and whether or not it was an investment-related business. In addition, the registrant must provide information on any active professional certifications, registrations currently held, outside business activities, and current employer's name, employment dates, office location, and registration information.

Fingerprinting of Securities Industry Personnel

Under Rule 17f-2 of the Securities Exchange Act of 1934, all partners, directors, officers, and employees of every member of a national securities exchange, broker, dealer, registered transfer agent, and registered clearing agency are required to be fingerprinted. The fingerprints are submitted to the United States Attorney General to be processed and maintained on file. There are some exceptions to this rule, however, such as employees who are not engaged in the sale of securities, employees who do not have regular access or do not regularly process securities or cash, and employees who do not have direct supervisory responsibility for employees with the responsibilities previously described. The importance of this requirement lies in the ability that it provides for the United States government and regulatory organizations to identify members' employees and to help to prevent fraudulent activity.

Broker and Dealer

Under the Securities Exchange Act of 1934, a "broker" is defined as "any person engaged in the business of effecting transactions in securities for the account of others." The Act does provide an important exception for banks, which typically transact in securities only through third-party brokerage arrangements, trust activities, or permissible securities transactions, such as those in commercial paper or exempted securities. "Dealer" is defined under the Act as "any person engaged in the business of buying and selling securities...for such person's own account through a broker or otherwise." Therefore, a broker acts as a middleman between two parties in a transaction, whereas a dealer takes one side of the transaction to buy or sell for his own account.

Security

A "security" is defined under the Securities Exchange Act of 1934 as "any note, stock, treasury stock, security future, security-based swap, bond, debenture, certificate of interest or participation in any profit-sharing agreement or in any oil, gas, or other mineral royalty or lease, any collateral-trust certificate, preorganization certificate or subscription, transferable share, investment contract, voting-trust certificate, certificate of deposit for a security, any put, call, straddle, option, or privilege on any security, certificate of deposit, or group or index of securities or any put, call, straddle, option or privilege entered into on a national exchange relating to a foreign currency, or in general, any instrument commonly known as a 'security.'" It is often easier to remember what is not a security. This group includes currency and any notes or banker's acceptances with maturities of less than nine months.

Persons Associated with a Broker or Dealer and Statutory Disqualification

Under the Securities Exchange Act of 1934, "persons associated with a broker or dealer" is defined as "any partner, officer, director, or branch manager of such broker or dealer (or any person occupying a similar status or performing similar functions), any person directly or indirectly controlling, controlled by, or under common control with such broker or dealer, or any employee of such broker or dealer, except that any person associated with a broker or dealer whose functions are solely clerical or ministerial shall not be included in the meaning of such term." The Act also states that a person is subject to a statutory disqualification if such person has been and is expelled or suspended from membership with a member firm or has been suspended or had membership revoked by a foreign financial regulatory authority, other domestic regulatory authority, or the Commodity Futures Trading Commission. Additionally, the Act provides for statutory disqualification if such person has associated with a member who has falls into the previously described category or has knowingly contributed to actions that could lead to such consequences.

Person Associated with a Member

A "person associated with a member" is defined in Article I of the FINRA By-Laws to mean "(1) a natural person who is registered or has applied for registration under the Rules of the Corporation; (2) a sole proprietor, partner, officer, director, or branch manager of a member, or other natural person occupying a similar status or performing similar functions, or a natural person engaged in the investment banking or securities business who is directly or indirectly controlling or controlled by a member, whether or not any such person is registered or exempt from registration with the Corporation under these By-Laws or the Rules of the Corporation; and (3) for purposes of Rule 8210, any other person listed in Schedule A of Form BD of a member." A clear understanding of this definition is important to be able to determine who is subject to the myriad rules and regulations imposed by FINRA.

Conditions Under Which Certain Persons Would Be Deemed Ineligible for Membership

According to Article III of the FINRA By-Laws, there are a number of circumstances that could lead to ineligibility for membership or association with FINRA, including failing or ceasing to satisfy the qualification requirements and becoming the subject of a disqualification. Additionally, a determination of ineligibility could result from not filing all required documentation and forms in a timely fashion. Individual persons are also subject to these same requirements or would also face ineligibility. Members who continue to associate with these ineligible persons may also face sanctions, up to a termination of membership. Once deemed ineligible, the member can file an application to the Board of FINRA requesting relief from the ineligibility and a continuation in membership.

Disqualification

Article III of the FINRA By-Laws defines a "disqualification" by pointing to the definition of "statutory disqualification" in Section 3(a)(39) of the Securities Exchange Act of 1934, which provides the following instances that would lead to such a disqualification:

- The person is expelled or suspended from membership or participation in any member of a self-regulatory organization (SRO), any SRO itself, foreign equivalent of SROs, foreign securities exchanges, contract markets, or futures associations
- The person is subject to an order of the SEC denying his status as a broker or dealer for a period not exceeding 12 months, or barring for a period of not more than 12 months the person's association with a broker or dealer
- Or has associated with a person or member who meets the above criteria

Article III of the FINRA By-Laws prohibits members from continuing to associate with any person who has been subject to a statutory disqualification. However, the By-Laws go on to further clarify that applicants who have been the subject of a statutory disqualification may request permission to continue working in the industry. The determination as to whether or not to allow this association occurs in an "eligibility proceeding." Once a FINRA member becomes aware of a statutory disqualification, it must take corrective action in one of two ways. First, the member could terminate the person subject to the statutory disqualification, which would require the submission of Form U5. Alternatively, the member may want to retain the person. In such an instance, the member would be required to file Form MC-400 along with an updated U4 showing the disqualifying event.

Membership

Article V of the FINRA By-Laws requires that an applicant by any person for registration with FINRA must include an agreement to comply with all federal securities laws, the rules of the Municipal Securities Rulemaking Board, and the Treasury Department – on top of all of the rules and laws of FINRA, NASD, and other self-regulatory operations. Additional such applicant information may include fingerprints, detailed business plans, financial statements, descriptions of any recordkeeping and supervisory systems to be utilized, and a description of the experience and qualifications of supervisors.

Under Article IV – Membership of the FINRA By-Laws, each FINRA member must appoint and certify one executive representative. This representative is responsible for voting and acting on behalf of that member in all FINRA-related affairs. More than one representative may represent a corporation through additional positions in a corporate office or on the board or committees. Members must give notice when their representative will be changing, but can temporarily allow a substitute of their representative if that substitute is a member of senior management and a registered principal. Executive representatives are responsible for maintaining updated contact information with FINRA, especially their email address.

Resignation of a Member

Article IV of the FINRA By-Laws, which details the specific requirements of FINRA membership, also specifies the proper steps to take for a member that wishes to voluntarily resign its membership. A member is free to resign membership at any time, but must do so through a formal resignation process. The resignation becomes effective as soon as (1) 30 days after receipt of the formal resignation request, (2) all of the member's indebtedness due to FINRA has been paid, and (3) no complaints or actions are pending against the member. FINRA has the authority to supersede these rules, however, and can declare a resignation effective at any time.

Termination of Membership

Article IV of the FINRA By-Laws states that a member's membership with the Corporation "shall terminate upon its liquidation, dissolution, or winding up, and the membership of a sole proprietor which is a member shall terminate at death, provided that all obligations of membership under the By-Laws and the Rules of the Corporation have been fulfilled." However, a merger, reorganization, consolidation, or name change will not result in termination so long as the resulting member maintains a presence in the securities or investment banking business and continues to meet all qualification requirements. Similar requirements exist for the continued membership of a partnership following the death, withdrawal, or addition of a new partner.

Branch Offices of Members

Pursuant to Article IV of the FINRA By-Laws, each branch office of a member is required to register with the Corporation. Additionally, these branch offices must pay all applicable dues, assessments, and other charges that are applicable to all members and outlined in these same By-Laws. Branch offices are required to have supervisory personnel on site and must ensure that any branch openings, branch closings, branch relocations, changes in supervisory personnel, or changes in branch activities must be reported to the Corporation within 30 days of such event. The scrutiny of branch offices as well as of headquarter locations is important to ensure that these same investment banking and securities job functions are supervised and regulated in the same way regardless of the physical location.

Information That Is Required of an Applicant for Registration

According to Article V of the FINRA By-Laws, an application for membership must include, at a minimum, "an agreement to comply with federal securities laws, the rules and regulations thereunder, the rules of the Municipal Securities Rulemaking Board and the Treasury Department, the By-Laws of the Corporation, NASD Regulation, and NASD Dispute Resolution, the Rules of the Corporation, and all rulings, orders, directions, and decisions issued and sanctions imposed under the rules of the Corporation." In addition, the Corporation may require any other information from the applicant deemed to be "reasonable" in helping it to determine the applicant's qualifications for application. If this information changes in any way, the application may be revised through the use of "supplementary amendments" that must be filed within 30 days. If the new information relates to the applicant's statutory disqualification, that amendment must be submitted within 10 days of the disqualification.

Registered Representatives and Associated Persons

Article V of the FINRA By-Laws prohibits any member from associating with another member or person and engaging in the investment banking or securities business until that member has determined whether or not the person satisfies the qualification requirements in Section 2 and is also not subject to a statutory disqualification. More specifically, Article III of the By-Laws gives the authority to the FINRA Board to determine the rules and regulations regarding training, competence, experience, and any other metrics on which to determine qualification. The requirements imposed by the FINRA Board may differ from one industry or sector of the financial markets to another.

Termination with a Member of an Associated Person

Within 30 days following the termination of an associated person, a member must give notice of the termination to FINRA. An additional copy of the notice provided to FINRA must also be provided to the terminated person. The provision within

FINRA's By-Laws relating to retention of jurisdiction simply means that even after a member or associated person has resigned or had membership cancelled or revoked, that former member or associated person will still be subject to the filing of a complaint under FINRA's rules for any actions taken by the member or associated person prior to the resignation, cancellation, or revocation of membership. However, complaints may only be filed for up to two years following the effective date of the resignation, cancellation, or revocation.

Conditions Under Which a Person Whose Association with a Member Has Been Terminated Can Be the Subject of the Filing of a Complaint

Article V of the FINRA By-Laws provides for three situations under which a person whose association with a member has been terminated can become the subject of a complaint. The complaint can be filed if:

- The complaint is filed within two years of the effective date of the termination. The two-year time period is reset for each actionable conduct under any applicable statute, rule, or regulation
- The complaint is filed within two years of the date on which registration was cancelled or revoked under the Corporation's rules
- A complaint is filed against an unregistered person within two years of the date on which that person's association with the member ceased

Individuals to Whom the FINRA Membership and Registration Rules Apply

According to FINRA Rule 1230, the membership and registration rules apply to any member of senior management with oversight of the functions described below, and any persons designated by senior management to approve or authorize work in the functions described below, or any persons with authority to commit the member or member's capital in the functions described below. Such covered functions include client on-boarding; collection, maintenance, re-investment, and disbursement of funds; receipt and delivery of securities; bank, custody, depository, and firm account management and reconciliation; settlement, fail control, buy-ins, segregation, possession, and control; trade confirmations and statements; margin; stock loans and securities lending; prime brokerage; approval of valuation pricing models; financial control; preparing and filing financial reports; defining and approving business requirements for sales and trading systems, business security requirements, and information entitlement policies; and posting entries to a member's books and records.

Groups That May Be Exempt from the Provisions of FINRA Rule 1230

FINRA Rule 1230 provides that a person who is or has within the prior two years been registered with FINRA under one of the positions mentioned below may be exempt from passing the Operations Professional qualification examination prior to registering to become registered as an Operations Professional. The exempt positions include an Investment Company/Variable Contracts Representative, General Securities Representative, U.K or Canada Securities Representative, Registered Options Principal, General Securities Sales Supervisor, Compliance

Officer, Supervisory Analyst, General Securities Principal, Investment Company Products/Variable Products Principal, Financial and Operations Principal, Introducing Broker-Dealer Financial and Operations Principal, and Municipal Fund Securities Principal or Limited Principal.

Membership, Registration, and Qualification Requirements

Under FINRA Rule 1000, all persons who meet the definition of a registered representative presented in FINRA Rule 1230 must apply for membership with FINRA. Such application includes the appointment of a supervisory principal, submission of a Form U4 (containing personal, educational, employment, and criminal history), filing of fingerprints, and any required qualification examinations. Furthermore, Rule 1000 goes on to require ongoing education and certification through the Regulatory and Firm Elements. The Regulatory Element is required annually by December 31. The Firm Element must be completed each year. Firms must maintain written training plans for the Firm Element and any registered person who fails to complete either required element may be subject to suspension or termination of membership.

Various Registration Categories

Under FINRA Rule 1230, subsections 1 through 5 and 7 through 14 have been reserved for future additions to the rules. However, Section 6 of Rule 1230 does offer further clarification with respect to the category of registered representatives known as operations professionals. The scope of functions for these operations professionals could span a number of roles, including client on-boarding; collection, maintenance, re-investment, and disbursement of funds; receipt and delivery of securities; bank, custody, depository, and firm account management and reconciliation; settlement, fail control, buy-ins, segregation, possession, and control; trade confirmations and statements; margin; stock loans and securities lending; prime brokerage; approval of valuation pricing models; financial control; preparing and filing financial reports; defining and approving business requirements for sales and trading systems, business security requirements, and information entitlement policies; and posting entries to a member's books and records. This category would also include those who supervise or delegate supervision of the functions mentioned above.

Consequences of a Failure to Complete the Requirements in a Timely Manner

FINRA Rule 1250 requires that registered persons must complete both a Regulatory Element and a Firm Element as part of ongoing continuing education. The Regulatory Element must be completed on the second anniversary of registration and every three years thereafter. The Firm Element must be completed at least annually. Failure to complete the Regulatory Element within 120 days of the anniversary date will result in that person's registration being deemed inactive, thus preventing that person from engaging in any duties or functions that require registration. After two years of inactive registration, a person's registration will be terminated. All persons covered under a member's written plan for the Firm

Element of continuing education are required to make every reasonable and appropriate effort to complete the firm's continuing education programs.

Requirements for a Registered Person Who Has Been Subject to Any Sanctions or Statutory Disqualifications

FINRA Rule 1250 provides that a person will be required to retake the Regulatory Element and satisfy all of its requirements if that person (1) has been the subject of any statutory disqualification, (2) has been suspended or fined more than $5,000 for any securities law or regulation violation or violation of the rules of any securities governing body or self-regulatory organization, or (3) has been ordered as part of a sanction from a self-regulatory organization or securities governmental agency to retake the Regulatory Element. This retaking of the Regulatory Element must occur within 120 days of the statutory disqualification or final decision of sanctions described above.

Regulatory and Firm Element Requirements

FINRA Rule 1250 requires members and associated persons to complete both a Regulatory Element and Firm Element as part of its continuing education program. The Regulatory Element must be completed within 120 days of the second anniversary of registration and within 120 days of each three-year anniversary thereafter. The Regulatory Element can be administered on site by the member so long as FINRA's provisions relating to principal in charge, site requirements, technology requirements, supervision, proctors, and administration are met. A letter of attestation must be provided upon completion and the member is also responsible for designating contact person(s) at the member who will be notified when it is approaching the time for a person to complete the Regulatory Element. The Firm Element must be outlined in a written plan by the member and must be completed at least once per year. The Firm Element must, at a minimum, cover general investment features and risk factors, suitability and sales practice considerations, regulatory requirements, and ethics and professional responsibility.

Reasons That Investment Advisers Are of National Concern

Under Section 201 of the Investment Advisers Act of 1940, investment advisers are of national concern because:

- "their advice, counsel, publications, writings, analyses and reports are furnished and distributed, and their contracts, subscription agreements, and other arrangements with clients are negotiated and performed, by the use of the mails and means and instrumentalities of interstate commerce"
- "their advice, counsel, publications, writings, analyses and reports customarily relate to the purchase and sale of securities traded on national securities exchanges and in interstate over-the-counter markets, securities issued by companies engaged in business in interstate commerce, and securities issued by national banks and member banks of the Federal Reserve System"

- "the foregoing transactions occur in such volume as substantially to affect interstate commerce, national securities exchanges, and other securities markets, the national banking system and the national economy"

Thus, investment advisers utilize means of interstate commerce, subjecting it to federal guidelines, and also consult and analyze such large and important transactions that their output could have a significant impact on other markets and the national economy.

INVESTMENT ADVISER

"Investment adviser" is defined within the Investment Advisers Act of 1940 as "any person who, for compensation, engages in the business of advising others, either directly or through publications or writings, as to the values of securities or as to the advisability of investing in, purchasing, or selling securities, or who, for compensation and as part of a regular business, issues or promulgates analyses or reports concerning securities." Notable exceptions to the definition of an investment adviser include banks and bank holding companies, lawyers, accountants, engineers and teachers, brokers and dealers who only perform those services incidentally to their normal course of business and receive no special compensation, publishers of newspapers, magazines and regular circulations, and persons whose advice or recommendations relate only to exempt securities, such as US treasuries.

INVESTMENT SUPERVISORY SERVICES AND PERSONS ASSOCIATED WITH AN INVESTMENT ADVISER

"Investment supervisory services" are defined within the Investment Advisers Act of 1940 to mean "the giving of continuous advice as to the investment of funds on the basis of the individual needs of each client." "Persons associated with an investment adviser" are defined as "any partner, officer, or director of such investment adviser (or any person performing similar functions), or any person directly or indirectly controlling or controlled by such investment adviser, including any employee of such investment adviser, except that for the purposes of Section 203 of this title, persons associated with an investment adviser whose functions are clerical or ministerial shall not be included in the meaning of such term."

REQUIREMENTS FOR REGISTRATION AS AN INVESTMENT ADVISER

Any investment adviser must file an application to become a registered investment advisor under the Investment Advisers Act of 1940. Such application process will include submission of the name and form of the organization, the principal office and branch offices, names of officers and directors, the educations and business affiliations for the past 10 years of all partners, officers, or directors, a description of the nature of the adviser's business, a balance sheet certified by an independent public accountant, whether and to what extent the adviser has discretion over clients' funds, and details around any disqualifications of the adviser. Within 45 days of filing, the SEC will either grant registration or initiate proceedings to further determine whether registration should be granted or denied. Until such time as registration is approved, the adviser is not allowed to perform any actions that are covered under the definition of a registered investment adviser, including using the mail or any means or interstate commerce to conduct its business.

Organizations that are exempt from registration under the Investment Advisers Act of 1940 include those investment advisers whose only clients are residents of the state in which the adviser maintains its principal office and does not advise on securities listed on national exchanges, advisers whose only clients are insurance companies, advisers whose only clients are foreign private advisers, advisers who are directors, trustees, officers, employees, or volunteers of a charitable organization, any plans in Section 414(e) of the Internal Revenue Code, and advisers who are registered with the Commodity Futures Trading Commission and whose business does not primarily consist of acting as an investment adviser.

Training of Representatives

Securities Act of 1933

The two objectives of the Securities Act of 1933 are to (i) "require that investors receive financial and other significant information concerning securities being offered for public sale" and (ii) "prohibit deceit, misrepresentations, and other fraud in the sale of securities." Issuing companies can meet these requirements by registering their securities. Registration requires that a company accurately disclose all relevant information concerning the business, the security being offered, company management, and the company's financial position. Without registration, it would be much more difficult for an investor to obtain all of the relevant information needed to make a sound and informed decision.

Offer to Sell, Dealer, and Registration Statement

The Securities Act of 1933 defines offer to sell as including "every attempt or offer to dispose of, or solicitation of an offer to buy, a security or interest in a security, for value." However, the Act does further clarify that an offer to sell does not include preliminary negotiations or agreements between an issuer and an underwriter who are in contract with an issuer. A dealer is defined within the Act as "any person who engages either for all or part of his time, directly or indirectly, as agent, broker, or principal, in the business of offering, buying, selling, or otherwise dealing or trading in securities issued by another person." Finally, registration statement "means the statement provided for in Section 6, and includes any amendment thereto and any report, document, or memorandum filed as part of such statement or incorporated therein by reference."

Issuer and Underwriter

The Securities Act of 1933 defines an issuer as "every person who issues or proposes to issue any security." Please bear in mind that person is defined as "an individual, a corporation, a partnership, an association, a joint-stock company, a trust, any unincorporated organization, or a government or political subdivision thereof." The issuer plays a key role in the securities markets because the return to the investor, whether through capital appreciation and dividends on equity securities or through coupon and principal repayments on debt securities, will be dependent on the financial performance of the issuer. An underwriter is defined as "any person who has purchased from an issuer with a view to, or offers or sells for an issuer with, the distribution of any security." Underwriters are primarily utilized by issuers in the primary distribution of securities. The role of the underwriter is to determine the initial pricing and to coordinate the sale and distribution of the security into the market. Underwriters are often also involved in the preparation of the necessary SEC filings and approvals.

Prospectus

The Securities Act of 1933 defines prospectus as "any prospectus, notice, circular, advertisement, letter, or communication, written or by radio or television, which offers any security for sale or confirms the sale of any security." The Act goes on to clarify that a notice, circular, letter, or advertisement is not considered to be a prospectus so long as it states from whom a prospectus can be obtained and does not do any more than identify the security and the price and state from whom orders will be executed. The purpose of the prospectus is to ensure that investors have access and are provided with, prior to the purchase of a security, a minimal level of information that is necessary for the investment decision-making process. Such information within the prospectus includes a mutual fund's objectives, strategy, risks, fees and expenses, and past performance. The format of each prospectus is the same to enable investors to easily compare different investments.

Insurance Company and Separate Account

As provided within the Securities Act of 1933, an insurance company is defined as "a company which is organized as an insurance company, whose primary and predominant business activity is the writing of insurance or the reinsuring of risks underwritten by insurance companies, and which is subject to supervision by the insurance commissioner, or a similar official or agency, of a State or territory or the District of Columbia; or any receiver or similar official or any liquidating agent for such company, in his capacity as such." A related term, a separate account, is defined within the Act as "an account established and maintained by an insurance company pursuant to the laws of any State or territory of the United States, the District of Columbia, or of Canada or any province thereof, under which income, gains and losses, whether or not realized, from assets allocated to such account, are, in accordance with the applicable contract, credited to or charged against such account without regard to other income, gains, or losses of the insurance company."

Investment Company Act of 1940

The Investment Company Act of 1940 intends to regulate investment companies, as such companies are considered to:

- Issue securities through interstate commerce that represent a large portion of all securities offered and traded and the national securities exchanges
- Invest, reinvest and trade securities through the national securities exchanges and interstate commerce, which comprise a significant portion of all trading activity
- Invest and trade in significant portions of securities issued by companies that engage in interstate commerce
- Act as a potential investment for a substantial part of the national savings, which affects the national economy and the flow of savings into the capital markets
- Engage in activities of interstate commerce across a geographically diverse group of stakeholders that cannot be effectively governed through state regulations

The purpose of the Act is to help to regulate such investment companies in order to protect investors.

Circumstances Under Which Investment Companies Can Adversely Affect the Interests of Investors

The Investment Company Act of 1940 outlines a number of ways in which the actions of investment companies could adversely affect investors if not properly regulated, including:

- Investors making decisions to buy, sell, or exchange securities without adequate information
- Investment companies that are managed for the benefit of their directors or officers rather than the holders of the security
- Securities issued by investment companies that fail to protect the privileges of its holders
- Inequitable or unduly concentrated control of investment companies
- Investment companies utilizing unsound or misleading methods of reporting
- Reorganization of investment companies without the consent of shareholders
- Excessive borrowing by investment companies that unduly increases the risk of more junior securities
- Investment companies operating without adequate reserves or assets

Advisory Board

Under the Investment Company Act of 1940, an investment company's advisory board is defined as "a board, whether elected or appointed, which is distinct from the board of directors or board of trustees, of an investment company, and which is comprised solely of persons who do not serve such company in any other capacity, whether or not the functions of such board are such as to render its members 'directors' within the definition of that term, which board has advisory functions as to investments but has no power to determine that any security or other investment shall be purchased or sold by such company."

Employees' Securities Company

An employees' securities company is defined within the Investment Company Act of 1940 as "any investment company or similar issuer all of the outstanding securities of which (other than short-term paper) are beneficially owned (A) by the employees or persons on retainer of a single employer or of two or more employers each of which is an affiliated company of the other, (B) by former employees of such employer or employers, (C) by members of the immediate family of such employees, persons on retainer, or former employees, (D) by any two or more of the foregoing classes of persons, or (E) by such employer or employers together with any one or more of the foregoing classes of persons."

Exchange and Face-Amount Certificate

The Investment Company Act of 1940 defines an exchange as "any organization, association, or group of persons, whether incorporated or unincorporated, which constitutes, maintains, or provides a market place or facilities for bringing together purchasers and sellers of securities or for otherwise performing with respect to securities the functions commonly performed by a stock exchange as that term is generally understood, and includes the market place and the market facilities maintained by such exchange." A face-amount certificate is defined within the Act as "any certificate, investment contract, or other security which represents an obligation on the part of its issuer to pay a stated or determinable date or dates more than twenty-four months after the date of issuance, in consideration of the payment of periodic installments of a stated or determinable amount (which security shall be known as a face-amount certificate of the 'installment type'); or any security which represents a similar obligation on the part of a face-amount certificate company, the consideration for which is the payment of a single lump sum (which security shall be known as a 'fully paid' face-amount certificate)."

Government Security and Investment Banker

The Investment Company Act of 1940 defines a government security as "any security issued or guaranteed as to principal or interest by the United States, or by a person controlled or supervised by and acting as an instrumentality of the Government of the United States pursuant to authority granted by the Congress of the United States; or any certificate of deposit for any of the foregoing." An investment banker is defined within the Act as "any person engaged in the business of underwriting securities issued by other persons, but does not include an investment company, any person who acts as an underwriter in isolated transactions but not as a part of a regular business, or any person solely by reason of the fact that such person is an underwriter for one or more investment companies."

Issuer, Periodic Payment Plan Certificate, and Promoter

The Investment Company Act of 1940 defines an issuer as "every person who issues or proposes to issue any security, or has outstanding any security which it has issued." A periodic payment plan certificate is defined within the Act as "(A) any certificate, investment contract, or other security providing for a series of periodic payments by the holder, and representing an undivided interest in certain specified securities or in a unit or fund of securities purchased wholly or partly with the proceeds of such payments, and (B) any security the issuer of which is also issuing securities of the character described in clause (A) and the holder of which has substantially the same rights and privileges as those which holders of securities of the character described in clause (A) have open completing the periodic payments for which such securities provide." Finally, a promoter of a company or proposed company is defined within the Act to mean "a person who, acting alone or in concert with other persons, is initiating or directing, or has within one year initiated or directed, the organization of such company."

Redeemable Security and Sales Load

The Investment Company Act of 1940 defines a redeemable security as "any security, other than short-term paper, under the terms of which the holder, upon its presentation to the issuer or to a person designated by the issuer, is entitled (whether absolutely or only out of surplus) to receive approximately his proportionate share of the issuer's current net assets, or the cash equivalent thereof." Additionally, a sales load is defined within the Act to be "the difference between the price of a security to the public and that portion of the proceeds from its sale which is received and invested or held for investment by the issuer (or in the case of a unit investment trust, by the depositor or trustee), less any portion of such difference deducted for trustee's or custodian's fee, insurance premiums, issue taxes, or administrative expenses or fees which are not properly chargeable to sales or promotional activities."

Business Development Company

The Investment Company Act of 1940 defines a business development company as "any closed-end company which – (A) is organized under the laws of, and has its principal place of business in, any State or States; (B) is operated for the purpose of making investments in securities described in paragraphs (1) through (3) of section 55(a), and makes available significant managerial assistance with respect to the issuers of such securities, provided that a business development company must make available significant managerial assistance only with respect to the companies which are treated by such business development company as satisfying the 70 per centum of the value of its total assets condition of section 55…; and (C) has elected pursuant to section 54(a) to be subject to the provisions of sections 55 through 65."

Qualified Purchaser

The Investment Company Act of 1940 defines a qualified purchaser as:

- Any natural person who owns at least $5,000,000 in investments
- Any company that owns at least $5,000,000 in investments that is owned by or for immediate relatives, including siblings, spouses, or lineal descendants
- Any trust, not established for the purpose of acquiring such securities, the trustees and decision makers of which meet the other classifications provided herein
- Any person, whether acting for itself or other qualified purchasers, who owns and has discretionary investment control over at least $25,000,000 in investments

The SEC maintains the right to determine the rules and regulations that should be applied to this class of investors.

Information That Must Be Provided Within the Application of an Investment Company

Section 8 of the Investment Company Act of 1940 prescribes the information that an investment company must provide to apply for registration. First, an investment company must indicate the extent to which it intends to conduct business in borrowing money, issuing senior securities, underwriting securities issued by others, investing in a concentrated manner in specific businesses or industries, buying/selling real estate or commodities, and making loans. Additionally, applicants must disclose portfolio turnover for each of the last three years and a recital of all investment policies. Finally, the applicant must provide the name and address of each affiliated person, the names and addresses of each other company with which the affiliated persons are officers, partners or directors, and a statement of the business experience for the preceding five years of each officer or director of the applicant.

Actions Deemed Unlawful for Registered Investment Companies to Engage In

Section 12 of the Investment Company Act of 1940 states that it is unlawful for registered investment companies to:

- Purchase a security on margin. The exception to this rule is that it is permissible for an investment company to purchase short-term credits on margin if they are necessary to clear certain transactions
- Participate on a joint basis in any securities trading account. The exception to this rule is that an investment company may participate in a joint trading account for a security in which the investment company is a participant in connection with the underwriting of such security
- Sell short any security, unless the short sale is in connection with the underwriting of the security and the investment company is a participant in the underwriting

Distribution of Shares by a Registered Open-End Management Investment Company

Section 22 of the Investment Company Act of 1940 states that registered open-end investment companies shall only issue securities for cash or other securities. Open-end investment companies are prohibited under this section of the Act from issuing securities for services or for property other than cash or securities. The only exception to this rule is a dividend or other distribution resulting from a reorganization. Additionally, the Act further states that open-end investment companies may not in any way restrict the transferability or negotiability of any security outside of the provisions of its registration statement or as allowed by the Commission.

Classes of Investment Companies

The three principal classes of investment companies as provided in the Investment Company Act of 1940 are as follows:

- Face-amount certificate company – an investment company that is engaged or proposes to engage in the business of issuing face-amount certificates of the installment type, or which has been engaged in such business and has any such certificate outstanding.
- Unit investment trust – an investment company that (A) is organized under a trust indenture, contract of custodianship or agency, or similar instrument, (B) does not have a board of directors, and (C) issues only redeemable securities, each of which represents an undivided interest in a unit of specified securities, but does not include a voting trust.
- Management company – any investment company other than a face-amount certificate company or a unit investment trust.

The Investment Company Act of 1940 provides for four subclassifications of management companies. Management companies can be subclassified as either open-end or closed-end companies and as either diversified or non-diversified companies.

An open-end company is a management company that is offering for sale or has outstanding redeemable securities of which it is the issuer. All management companies not fitting this profile are classified as closed-end companies. Securities of closed-end companies can only be purchased on the secondary market and are not available directly from the issuing company.

Management companies are classified as diversified when the following three conditions are met:

- At least 75 percent of the company's total assets comprises cash, government securities, and securities of other investment companies.
- Securities from any one issuer do not represent more than 5 percent of the management company's total assets.

- Any securities held by the management company do not represent more than 10 percent of the outstanding voting securities of a given issuer.
- All management companies not meeting these three criteria are considered to be non-diversified.

The Price at Which Any Offer of Exchange Must Be Made

Section 11 of the Investment Company Act of 1940 stipulates that any offer of exchange between a registered open-end investment company or principal underwriter of an open-end investment company and the holder of a security must be based on the relative net asset values of the securities to be exchanged, unless preapproved by the Commission. The net asset value to be used in this determination is further clarified to be calculated at either the time the offeror receives acceptance of the offer or at any later time that may be specified in the offer. Additionally, the Act further clarifies that this provision does not apply to an offer by a principal underwriter to an individual investor in the course of retail business.

Rules Governing an Offer of Exchange

Section 11 of the Investment Company Act of 1940 stipulates that any offer of exchange between a registered open-end investment company or principal underwriter of an open-end investment company and the holder of a security must be based on the relative net asset values of the securities to be exchanged. This provision applies to any offer of exchange between a security of an open-end investment company and a security of a unit investment trust or face-amount certificate company. Additionally, the provision also applies to an offer of exchange of unit investment trusts or face-amount certificates for securities of any other investment company. The one exception to this provision is in the case of a reorganization that required a majority vote of the shareholders.

Actions That Require a Majority Vote of Outstanding Voting Securities

Section 13 of the Investment Company Act of 1940 stipulates four activities that cannot be taken by registered investment companies without a majority vote of shareholders, including:

- Changing from a diversified to a non-diversified company
- Borrowing money, issuing senior securities, underwriting securities of other companies, transacting in real estate or commodities, and making loans to other people, unless explicitly permitted in its registration statement
- Straying from written policies with respect to concentration of investments in particular industries, or from any other policies that require a majority vote of shareholders
- Changing the nature of its business so that it is no longer considered to be an investment company

Criteria That an Investment Advisory Service Offering Must Meet to Not Be Deemed an Investment Company

Rule 3a-4 of the Investment Company Act of 1940 provides for important exemptions from the definition of an investment company for the provision of discretionary investment advisory services to clients. In order to qualify for the exemption, the offering must meet the following qualifications:

- Each client's account is managed strictly within that client's financial goals and investment objectives, including any reasonable restrictions the client has imposed on the manager.
- The discretionary manager must thoroughly document the client's suitability at the opening of the account and update the information at least annually, with further quarterly contacts by the manager to inquire about changing financial circumstances or new restrictions.
- Clients maintain the ability to impose restrictions on management of the account, including types of securities to be purchased or held.
- Each client receives a quarterly account statement detailing any transactions, contributions, withdrawals, fees, and beginning and ending values.
- Each client has the right to withdraw funds, vote securities or delegate votes, and receive written transaction confirmations.

529 Plan and Education Savings Plans

A Section 529 College Savings Plan is a valuable tool for parents to invest funds on a tax-preferred basis to be used for the costs of college education. Contributions into the plan are made with after-tax dollars, so the benefit of the plan is not experienced at the time of contribution. However, your contributions grow tax-free and can be invested as you choose to allocate the funds within the options available in your specific plan. The funds can be withdrawn to cover any "qualified higher education expenses," including tuition, room and board, and books and computers. The Tax Cuts and Jobs Act (TCJA) also permitted 529 funds to go towards K-12 expenses, and the SECURE Act of 2019 permitted them to pay up to $10,000 in student loan debt. While the contribution limits vary by plan and the state or institution offering the plan, often times the contribution limit is in excess of $200,000. Some Section 529 Plans also offer a "prepaid" option, in which the owner of the account will commit to certain payments over a period of time up until the date at which the child is expected to enter the higher education institution. This option essentially "locks in" college costs and moves the investment risk of the funds back to the sponsoring institution.

Section 529 College Savings Plans and Coverdell Education Savings Plans function in much the same manner, but also have a number of key differences with respect to the use of the funds and contribution limits. Both types of accounts allow for individuals to make after-tax contributions, which are invested and grow tax-free until the tax-free distribution of the funds for "qualified expenses." This definition of *qualified expenses* is one source of difference, though the difference is smaller due to the Tax Cuts & Jobs Act (TCJA). Pre-TCJA, 529 plans could not pay for K-12 expenses, but post-TCJA, 529 plans (as well as ESAs) can. 529 plans are limited to $10,000 and to K-12 *tuition*, however, while ESAs have no limit and can also go towards other related K-12 expenses, e.g. books, supplies, and uniforms. Additionally, Section 529 plans allow for significantly higher contributions, when compared to the $2,000 annual limit on contributions into a Coverdell account, and Section 529 Plans also do not impose income limits on the amount of contributions.

Fees Borne by the Account Holder in a 529 Plan

Fees within 529 plans can come from a number of sources and may include sales charges (for programs bought through a broker), management expenses, and administrative costs. 529 plans may be purchased either directly from the plan administrator or through a financial adviser. Plans sold through financial advisers, while providing for additional services related to the adviser's investment expertise, will typically have significant sales charges that can detract from the overall return of the portfolio. Most plans sold directly through the administrator offer tools that help investors determine their appropriate asset allocation based on their risk tolerance and time horizon. In addition to sales charges, all plans impose fees for the management of the underlying investment options. This is one area where research and due diligence in comparing all available plans may yield cost savings. Additionally, many plans offer options for both active and passive investment management. Passive management will track an index and lower the expense ratios of the plan. Finally, most plans impose a minimal administrative fee to cover the cost of statements and reporting.

Qualified Retirement Plan

A retirement plan is referred to as "qualified" when it meets certain criteria as specified within the Internal Revenue Code and as a result is subject to beneficial tax treatment on contributions, distributions, and/or investment gains. The Internal Revenue Code specifies criteria relating to eligibility, matching contributions, vesting, and the timing of distributions. Examples of qualified plans include a 401(k) plan, a Roth IRA, and a Keogh plan. A 401(k) plan, which is a company-sponsored retirement plan, provides for the pre-tax deferral of earned income and the tax deferral of investment earnings within the plan. Upon reaching age 59 ½, participants can begin taking distributions from the plan that are taxed as ordinary income. Contribution limits, eligibility requirements, and vesting limitations are all determined by the provisions of the IRC. Another type of qualified plan is a Roth IRA, in which an investor contributes after-tax dollars into an account that grows tax-free and is ultimately received through a tax-free distribution. As with all other qualified plans, the IRC sets forth limitations on annual contributions and distribution timing.

Traditional and Roth IRA

In order to contribute to a traditional IRA, an individual who also participates in a company-sponsored retirement plan must fall below certain income limits (for 2026 – permitted contributions begin to phase out at $81,000 for singles and $129,000 for married couples, and are eliminated at $91,000 for singles and $149,000 for married couples). The 2026 contribution limit to traditional IRA accounts is $7,500. However, for those investors age 50 and over, the contribution limit is raised to $8,600.

In order to contribute to a Roth IRA, an individual must fall below certain income limits (for 2026 – permitted contributions begin to phase out at $153,000 for singles and $242,000 for married couples, and are eliminated at $168,000 for singles and $252,000 for married couples). The 2026 contribution limit to Roth IRA accounts is $7,500. However, for those investors age 50 and over, the contribution limit is raised to $8,600.

In both traditional and Roth IRA accounts, distributions to participants before age 59 ½ are considered to be early distributions and the account holder must pay an additional 10 percent tax. In a traditional IRA account, the IRS imposes certain minimum, or mandatory, distributions beginning at age 72. The amount of the minimum distribution is calculated as the account balance as of December 31 of the prior year divided by a factor provided by the IRS Uniform Lifetime Table. Roth IRAs differ in that no minimum or mandatory distributions are required prior to the death of the owner of the account. Upon the death of the account owner, the beneficiary has a number of options with respect to any remaining payments from the plan, including continuing to calculate the required minimum distribution based on the decedent's age, calculating the new required minimum distribution based on his or her own age, and withdrawing the entire remaining balance in a lump sum.

Education IRA and Coverdell Education Savings Account

A Coverdell Education Savings Account is a type of tax-advantaged investment account that allows parents the opportunity to save for educational expenses. Contributions into the plan are not tax-deductible and are limited to $2,000 per year (2026) for a given beneficiary. Additional limits may apply to the contributions that can be made to an account depending upon the modified adjusted gross income of the individual making the contribution. Amounts in the account grow tax-free and can be withdrawn tax-free as long as they are used for any qualified educational expenses at any eligible primary, secondary, or higher education institution. Educational expenses such as books, room and board, and computers are also covered as qualified expenses. Any amounts remaining in the account when the beneficiary of the account reaches age 30 must either be distributed (with gains subject to a 10 percent penalty) or rolled over into the account of another family member.

Simplified Employee Pension (SEP) Plan

Simplified Employee Pension (SEP) plans provide a nice alternative for small businesses and self-employed individuals who may not have the time or resources to adequately establish a traditional qualified retirement plan for employees like a 401(k). SEPs allow the employer to contribute funds to a tax-deferred account on behalf of employees. Unlike other types of plans, however, only the employer may contribute. The maximum contribution an employer can make to the account in any given tax year is 25 percent of an employee's pay. A business of any size may establish a SEP and all employees are eligible to participate. Distributions are treated as ordinary income once paid. These plans are especially attractive to employers as they are easier to adopt, require less administrative burden to operate, and do not impose the same filing requirements as other qualified plans.

SIMPLE

A Savings Incentive Match Plan for Employees (SIMPLE) offers the opportunity for small employers, defined as 100 employees or fewer, to provide a tax-deferred retirement savings tool into which employees can elect to contribute their income and employers must make matching or other contributions. Contributions to a SIMPLE are put into an Individual Retirement Account (IRA) for each employee and the IRAs follow all of the same taxation and distribution restrictions as for a traditional IRA. In 2026, employees under age 50 are allowed to contribute up to $17,000 into a SIMPLE and employees age 50 and older are allowed to contribute up to $21,000. Employer contributions must take the form of either a dollar-for-dollar match up to 3 percent of the employee's compensation or a non-elective contribution equal to 2 percent of the employee's compensation.

Keogh Plan

A Keogh plan allows self-employed individuals to save for retirement on a tax-deferred basis. However, a number of limitations apply to who can participate, how much participants can contribute, and how those contributions, and eventual distributions, are taxed. Much like a 401(k) plan, a Keogh is considered to be a "qualified" plan in that it is covered under Internal Revenue Code Section 401(a). As such, contributions to the plan made by the participant are tax-deductible. Once you begin receiving distributions from the plan, those distributions are taxed as ordinary income just as in other qualified plans. In order to be eligible to participate in a Keogh, you must be self-employed, a small business owner, or a sole proprietor. Working for a company does not preclude you from being eligible, so long as you also meet one of the previously mentioned criteria. Because participants are self-employed, the contribution limits to Keogh plans are higher than for many other qualified plans. Keogh plans limit contributions in a given tax year to 25 percent of your earned income, which is income less expenses arising from your self-employment activities.

Corporate Defined Benefit and Defined Contribution Retirement Plans

Defined benefit plans, which were especially popular throughout the last several decades, are arrangements between employers and employees under which the employer agrees to pay the employee a specific benefit, often a percentage of salary based on years of service, upon a qualifying retirement or termination event. Under such an arrangement, the employer is subject to the investment risk of having to set aside enough funds in order to be able to pay the promised benefits. Defined contribution plans, on the other hand, provide for a specific dollar amount or percentage of salary to be contributed to an employee's account. From that point forward, the investment of those funds is the responsibility of the employee and it is up to that employee to ensure that adequate funds are available to provide for retirement income.

Over the last several decades, employers have trended towards the use of defined contribution plans over defined benefit plans. Under a defined contribution plan, the employer agrees to make a certain contribution to the employee's retirement account, but at that point it becomes the responsibility of the employee to properly invest those funds to ensure he has enough income to meet his retirement needs. When compared to a defined benefit arrangement, in which the employer agrees to pay the employee a specified percentage of salary in retirement, the defined contribution arrangement provides more flexibility to employees to control their own investments. However, along with this control comes the investment risk that employers had assumed under defined benefit plans. Employers have also trended towards the defined contribution approach as it greatly simplifies the accounting and lowers the cost of providing retirement benefits.

403(b) Plan

A 403(b) plan is utilized by employers who are public educational institutions, churches, or non-profit organizations exempt under 501(c)(3). A 403(b)(7) plan is a specific subset that provides for individual custodial accounts made up of mutual funds. With each of these types of plans, if anyone is allowed to elect to defer compensation, then all participants must be allowed to defer. Participant deferrals into these plans are tax-deductible and accumulate tax-deferred. Distributions can be taken by participants upon reaching age 59 ½ or upon ending employment, suffering a hardship, or becoming disabled. Once distributions are taken from the plan they are taxed as ordinary income. The limitations on elective deferrals are the same as those for a 401(k) plan and may not exceed $24,500 (2026). In total, employee and employer contributions to the plan cannot exceed $72,000.

457 Plan

There are two types of 457 plans: 457(b) plans and 457(f) plans. The key difference between the two is that 457(b) plans are qualified under the Internal Revenue Code and eligible for favorable tax treatment while 457(f) plans are not. The only organizations that are permitted to offer 457 plans include state or local governments and tax-exempt 501(c) organizations. As with the other qualified plans, contributions to a 457(b) plan are tax-deductible and grow tax-deferred within the account until the time of distribution, at which time they are taxed as ordinary income. Employer and employee contributions are limited to $24,500 for employees under age 50 and $32,500 for employees age 50 and older (2026).

ERISA

The Employee Retirement Income Security Act of 1974 (ERISA) was enacted to provide minimum standards for pension plans established by employers. One such minimum standard relates to participation, as ERISA provides that the only employees who can be excluded from participation are those under the age of 21 and those who have not yet completed one full year of service with the employer.

The Act also provides that benefits must vest for participants upon attainment of normal retirement age, which is the earlier of the plan definition or age 65 with five years of service. The Act provides for two possible vesting schedules that can be applied to the employer's contributions under the plan – a five-year cliff schedule, in which the employee's vesting percentage is 0 until the fifth year, or a graded schedule in which the employee vests 20% for each completed year of service.

Contribution/Funding Requirements, Fiduciary Responsibilities

The Employee Retirement Income Security Act of 1974 (ERISA) was enacted to provide minimum standards for pension plans established by employers. One such minimum standard relates to minimum plan funding levels and states that plans must maintain sufficient assets to meet benefit obligations, as calculated given current interest rate and mortality assumptions. These requirements, and the steps required to bring the funding into compliance, vary depending on a number of plan- and employer-specific characteristics. The Act also imposes fiduciary responsibilities on anyone who has discretionary authority or management of the plan or renders fee-for-service investment advice regarding plan assets. These fiduciary responsibilities include a duty of loyalty to plan participants and beneficiaries, a duty of prudence in the management of plan assets, a duty to diversify investments as a risk-mitigation tool, and a duty to act in accordance with the terms of the plan document and to avoid entering into certain prohibited transactions.

Suitability Restriction of Investments, Prohibited Transactions and Penalties

The Employee Retirement Income Security Act of 1974 (ERISA) stipulates the prudent man standard of care with respect to plan fiduciaries. Included within that stipulation is the requirement that fiduciaries act solely in the interest of plan participants to defray reasonable expenses of administering the plan and diversifying the investments within the plan to minimize the risk of large losses. It is these requirements that guide the fiduciary in the selection of plan investments. Additionally, fiduciaries may not utilize the assets of the plan for their benefit or receive any consideration in connection with a transaction involving assets of the plan. Further restrictions involve transactions between the plan and a party in interest and transfers of property to the plan by a party in interest. Finally, ERISA outlines the criminal penalties available for a breach of this fiduciary duty or for an administrator that has failed to perform its duties.

Distribution/Withdrawal Rules That Apply to Tax-Qualified Retirement Plans

The Employee Retirement Income Security Act of 1974 (ERISA) establishes certain requirements with respect to the timing of distributions from retirement plans. For instance, tax-qualified plans such as a 401(k) or IRA allow a participant to begin taking distributions from the plan upon reaching age 59 ½. Any distributions taken prior to that time are subject to ordinary taxation plus an additional 10% penalty. The IRS also imposes certain minimum, or mandatory, distributions from these accounts beginning at age 72. The amount of the minimum distribution is calculated as the account balance as of December 31 of the prior year divided by a factor provided by the IRS Uniform Lifetime Table. Roth IRAs differ in that no minimum or mandatory distributions are required prior to the death of the owner of the account.

Transfer of an Individual's Retirement Plan Assets from an Employer-Sponsored Plan

Assets from a qualified plan, such as a 401(k), can be rolled over into a number of other accounts, including a traditional IRA or Roth IRA, a SEP, a 457(b) plan, another employer's 401(k) plan, or a 403(b) plan. These assets cannot, however, be rolled over into a SIMPLE IRA. Assets from a 403(b) or 457(b) plan can also be rolled over into a traditional IRA or Roth IRA, a SEP, another employer's 403(b) or 457(b) plan, or a 401(k) plan. As with qualified plan assets, these assets cannot be rolled over into a SIMPLE IRA. Finally, SEP IRAs and SIMPLE IRAs can be rolled over into a traditional IRA or Roth IRA, another employer's SEP, a 403(b) or 457(b) plan, or a 401(k) plan. However, only a SIMPLE can be rolled over into another employer's SIMPLE.

Non-Qualified Plan

Non-qualified deferred compensation plans allow a select group of management and highly compensated employees the opportunity to defer income on a pre-tax basis. In order to maintain its exemption from the Employee Retirement Income Security Act of 1974 (ERISA), these plans must remain unfunded. In the event of company insolvency, a participant in a non-qualified plan will be a general unsecured creditor of the company. Non-qualified deferred compensation plans differ from a 401(k) plan in a number of respects, including the ability to withdraw funds prior to age 59 ½ without an early withdrawal penalty, no IRS limitations on the amounts that can be contributed, and balances may not be rolled over into an IRA. Benefit payments made to participants are taxed as ordinary income when received. Following a number of corporate scandals, Internal Revenue Code Section 409A was enacted as part of the American Jobs Creation Act in 2004, restricting a participant's ability to modify, and more specifically to accelerate, the time and form of payment previously elected.

Deferral of Compensation and Deferral of Income Tax

Within a non-qualified deferred compensation plan, an employee's deferrals of compensation are not taxed as income. However, it is important to note that FICA taxes (Social Security and Medicare) are still taken from the employee's pay at the time of deferral. The notional account into which the employee has deferred compensation grows tax-deferred until the time of distribution. At the time of distribution, the payment is treated as ordinary income. However, since FICA was collected at the time of deferral, the distribution is not subject to FICA. For the plan sponsor of a non-qualified deferred compensation plan, there is a lost tax deduction because the income was never actually paid to the employee. However, the company must recognize an immediate liability on its balance sheet equal to the amount of the deferral. There is an additional balance sheet item to represent the future tax deferral that will be credited upon payment of the benefit to the participant, so this lost tax deduction is only a cash flow concern.

Impact of ERISA and Internal Revenue Code Section 409A on Non-Qualified Deferred Compensation

In order to avoid having to comply with the eligibility requirements of ERISA, non-qualified deferred compensation plans must remain unfunded, so that in the event of the insolvency of the plan sponsor, the employee would be a general creditor. As a result, non-qualified deferred compensation plans are typically offered to only a select group of management and other highly compensated employees, typically representing 10 percent or less of the total workforce. As a result of much of the scrutiny of executive pay following certain high-profile incidents (i.e., Enron, WorldCom, etc.), legislation was passed to enact Internal Revenue Code Section 409A, which imposed more stringent limitations around the timing and modification of distribution elections under a non-qualified plan. Section 409A specifies only a handful of distribution events under which a participant can receive payment, including separation from service, change in control, death, disability, and financial hardship. Additionally, the timing and form of payment must be specified prior to the deferral of the compensation. Code Section 409A also limits modifications so that any new payment timing submitted must be elected at least 12 months prior to the previously scheduled date of payment and must delay payment by at least five years from the originally scheduled date.

Conditions That Must Be Met Within a Non-Qualified Plan in Order to Qualify for Exemption from Certain ERISA Standards

In order to qualify for exemption from some of the more restrictive ERISA standards, a non-qualified plan's eligibility is limited to a "select group of management and highly compensated employees." This broad definition is open to interpretation and there is not a clear consensus as to the percentage of the workforce to which this equates, but 10-15 percent is typically considered the maximum range. In addition to the percentage of the workforce the eligible group represents, other factors that the Department of Labor considers include the compensation of the eligible group relative to the overall employee population and the compensation negotiating power of the eligible group. Additional guidance from the DOL has also indicated that the eligible group should only include those employees who have significant enough influence within the company to influence the design or administration of the plan.

Section 22 of the Investment Company Act of 1940

Section 22 of the Investment Company Act of 1940 stipulates how investment company securities must be priced in exchanges with investors and other investment companies. The Act gives registered securities associations the right to stipulate minimum and maximum transaction prices and minimum holding periods for securities. This authority is important to individual investors and other market participants because it largely eliminates, or at least reduces, any dilution of the value of such covered securities or any other unfair result to existing security holders of a purchase, sale, or redemption. Furthermore, any transactions between investment companies in a new issue must be made at a level approximately in line with the public offering price of such security that other market participants would expect to pay.

Distribution, Redemption, and Repurchase of Redeemable Securities

Section 22 of the Investment Company Act of 1940 – Distribution, Redemption, and Repurchase of Redeemable Securities – establishes important limitations around the methods for pricing transactions and redemption and exchange of investment company securities. These provisions are important to investors, as they protect current holders of securities from any transactions that would otherwise dilute the value of their holdings or limit their ability to redeem or exchange such securities. This is achieved through the requirement that transactions be affected at the net asset value of the security and with sales loads that are calculated according to a prescribed and consistent methodology. Additionally, it requires that any conditions for limiting redemption or exchange be explicitly outlined in the security's registration statement.

Pricing of Redeemable Securities at Distribution, Redemption, and Repurchase

Section 22 of the Investment Company Act of 1940 stipulates how investment company securities must be priced in exchanges with investors and other investment companies. Specifically, it grants registered securities associations the authority to dictate a method for computing the minimum price at which a redeemable security may be purchased from an investment company and the maximum price at which the member may sell a redeemable security to an investment company – both of which must relate to the security's net asset value. Additionally, these registered securities associations can also dictate a minimum time period that must elapse before the security can be sold or redeemed back to the investment company.

Persons to or Through Whom Redeemable Securities May Be Sold

Section 22 of the Investment Company Act of 1940 states that "No registered investment company shall sell any redeemable security issued by it to any person except either to or through a principal underwriter for distribution or at a current public offering price described in the prospectus." For a security that is currently being sold to the public through the use of an underwriter, the security can only be sold at a current public offering price described in the prospectus. The exceptions to this rule are sales to a dealer, the principal underwriter, or the issuer, and dividend payments or other distributions made only to registered holders of the security in proportion to their existing holdings or the size of the cash distribution.

Conditions Under Which a Registered Investment Company Is Able to Suspend the Right of Redemption or Postpone Payment

Section 22 of the Investment Company Act of 1940 permits a registered investment company to postpone payment or redemption for securities for three reasons, including:

- During a time in which the New York Stock Exchange is closed or during which trading is restricted, other than customary closings such as holidays and weekends.
- During any emergency period in which either disposal by the company is not reasonably practicable or the company cannot reasonably determine the fair value of its net assets.
- During any other period which the Commission believes will protect the security holders.

With the exception of the circumstances listed above, investment companies must accept redemption and transmit payment to security holders in a reasonable time frame pursuant to the other provisions of Section 22.

FINRA Requirements with Respect to the Annual Compliance Meeting

FINRA Rule 3130, in addition to requiring the designation of a chief compliance officer, also requires that chief compliance officer to meet at least once each year with the chief executive officer to ensure compliance with each of the following tasks:

- Ensure that the company establishes and maintains policies and procedures that comply with FINRA and MSRB rules and all other applicable securities laws and regulations, which may need to be modified as market and legislative events warrant.
- Review the annual compliance report.
- Consult with any outside consultants, lawyers, and/or accountants, in conjunction with both the chief compliance officer and chief executive officer as needed, to attest to the statements made in the annual compliance report.

FINRA Rule 1250

FINRA Rule 1250 stipulates that all persons associated with members must complete both a Regulatory Element and Firm Element of continuing education. It is the firm's responsibility to ensure that all registered persons complete, or make every reasonable effort to complete, the Firm Element. The Regulatory Element, which must be completed on the second anniversary of registration and every three years thereafter, is the responsibility of the registered person, but most firms have compliance departments that ensure all required continuing education is completed in a timely manner. If the Regulatory Element is not completed within 120 days of the anniversary date on which the Regulatory Element was to be completed, the person's registration will be deemed inactive, which means that individual cannot act in his capacity as a registered person. After two years of being inactive, a registration will be cancelled and that member will need to complete the entire application and registration process in order to regain association with a member.

Regulatory Element of Continuing Education

FINRA Rule 1250 states that every registered person must complete the required Regulatory Element of continuing education on the second anniversary of his registration date and every three years thereafter. If the registered person has not yet completed the Regulatory Element within 120 days following the anniversary date, also known as the base date, his registration will become inactive until the Regulatory Element is completed. After two years of being inactive, the registration will expire and the registered person will need to complete the full registration process once again to become registered. Rule 1250 also stipulates that a member can provide for in-house delivery of the Regulatory Element, provided that requirements with respect to the site of delivery, supervision, technology, and proctors are met. Finally, Rule 1250 requires the member to name a point of contact for correspondence regarding Regulatory Element requirements.

Firm Element of Continuing Education

FINRA Rule 1250 requires completion of the Firm Element portion of continuing education for any registered person who has direct contact with customers involving securities sales, trading, or investment banking, operations professionals, research analysts, and anyone who supervises individuals in one or more of these positions. The content of the Firm Element training must at a minimum relate to general investment features including risk factors, suitability and sales practices, regulatory requirements, and ethics and professional responsibility. Each member is responsible for developing a specific, written training plan for the Firm Element, though FINRA may require the training to include certain topics for all or a portion of the registered persons.

Supervises Associated Persons and Oversees Sales Practices

Supervision

NASD Rule 3010

NASD Rule 3010 stipulates the following requirements for a member's supervisory systems:

- The supervisory system must include a written set of procedures, which must be maintained over time.
- An appropriately registered principal, within each line of business in which the member is engaged and for which the member must be registered, must be appointed and assigned the authority to execute supervisory responsibilities.
- An office of supervisory jurisdiction (OSJ) must be appointed for each location as needed to supervise registered representatives and principals, especially when the registered persons at the location to be covered have regular contact with customers, where a significant number of registered representatives conduct their business, when the location of the office is geographically distant from another OSJ, when the registered representatives are geographically dispersed, and when the securities activities are diverse or complex.
- At least one designated registered principal in each OSJ and in the main office and at least one registered person in non-OSJ branches who can execute supervisory responsibilities of that office.
- Each registered person must be assigned to a registered representative or principal who will supervise that person.
- Each member must make reasonable efforts to ensure that all supervisory personnel are qualified through their experience or training.
- Each registered representative and principal must participate in a compliance meeting or discussion at least annually. The rule does not stipulate the location at which this meeting must occur.

NASD Rule 3010 – Supervision provides specific guidance for member firms with respect to the supervisory systems and written procedures that must be maintained. A member's supervisory system must provide for the establishment and maintenance of written procedures that:

- Include the designation of an appropriately registered principal who has the authority to carry out the supervisory responsibilities of the member for each type of business in which it engages and for which registration as a broker-dealer is required

- Designation of offices of supervisory jurisdiction (OSJs), considering whether registered persons at the locations engage in retail sales or other interaction with public customers, whether a substantial number of registered persons conduct business from those locations, whether the locations are separated geographically from other OSJs, whether the member's registered persons are geographically dispersed, and whether the securities at the locations are complex and/or diverse.

Additionally, each registered person must be assigned to a registered representative or principal who will be responsible for supervising that person's activities, the member firm must make reasonable efforts to ensure that all supervisory personnel are qualified to carry out their duties, and each registered representative and registered principal must take part in a meeting to discuss relevant compliance matters at least once annually.

Information About the Supervisory Personnel That Is to Be Included in the Written Procedures

NASD Rule 3010 provides detailed guidance regarding the specific policies and procedures that must be implemented by member firms to remain compliant with respect to supervisory practices. Included within that guidance is the information that member firms must maintain with respect to any supervisory personnel. More specifically, NASD Rule 3010 requires member firms to include within their supervisory procedures the titles, registrations, and locations of all supervisory personnel. The Rule additionally states that the written procedures contain the specific responsibilities of each registered individual in the context of all applicable securities laws and regulations. The member must ensure that the records properly reflect the beginning and ending effective dates for each supervisor, and these records must be maintained for at least three years, with the first two years being maintained in a readily accessible location.

Review of Supervisory Procedures

NASD Rule 3010 stipulates that members must conduct an internal review not less than annually. The review must cover all of the businesses in which the member engages and is intended to assist that member in identifying and preventing violations of securities laws and regulations. More specifically, the topics that must be covered in the member's written report include safeguarding of customers' funds, maintaining books and records, supervision of customer accounts by branch managers, transmittal of customers' funds, and validation of changes in customers' address and account information. Any branch office that supervises any non-branch locations and any office of supervisory jurisdiction must be inspected at least annually. Branch offices without supervisory responsibilities and non-branch locations only require inspection once every three years.

Supervision of Registered Representatives

NASD Rule 3010 stipulates that "Each member shall establish procedures for the review and endorsement by a registered principal in writing, on an internal record, of all transactions and for the review by a registered principal of incoming and outgoing written and electronic correspondence of its registered representatives with the public relating to the investment banking or securities business of such member." The rule further requires these procedures to be included in the written supervisory procedures and to be reasonably sufficient to provide adequate supervision of registered representatives of the member. This supervision of registered representatives is an important safeguard for the investing public, as correspondence coming from a member firm can be reasonably expected to have been reviewed by both the registered representative who created it as well as the registered principal, thus limiting the possibility of unethical actions.

Duty by a Member to Investigate the Qualifications of Applicants

Each member, prior to making a certification on an applicant's behalf in the registration process, must investigate the "good character, business repute, qualifications and experience" of such applicant. Such investigation must include, within 60 days of the registration application, a review of the applicant's Form U-5 if that applicant has previously been employed with a member firm. In addition to the Form U-5, a member must also investigate and review the applicant's Form 8-T if that individual has previously been registered with a registered futures association. This review by the member firm shifts responsibility for investigating the applicant's background from the association to the member firm, which is logical given that the applicant will be representing the member firm in the course of its business and the member firm will also have responsibility for the applicant's actions once registered and associated with the member.

Proper Training and Required Qualifications of Supervisory Personnel

NASD Rule 3010 states that member firms must make "Reasonable efforts to determine that all supervisory personnel are qualified by virtue of experience or training to carry out their assigned responsibilities." This is without question one of the least specific areas of guidance within the rules related to supervision. Due to the varied nature of businesses that could be engaged in the securities and investment banking industries and also the varied nature of roles that may require supervisory personnel, it would have been difficult for the regulators to more specifically determine what constitutes the amount of experience or education deemed to be qualified. Thus, the regulators have left it in the hands of the member firms to ensure, and to be able to justify, that their supervisory personnel have the industry experience and knowledge necessary to provide adequate supervision to registered representatives. Member firms are also incentivized to ensure that their supervisory procedures are executed, as they are ultimately responsible for the actions of their representatives.

Annual Compliance Meeting Required and the Parties Who Are Required to Attend

NASD Rule 3010 requires "The participation of each registered representative and registered principal, either individually or collectively, no less than annually, in an interview or meeting conducted by persons designated by the member at which compliance matters relevant to the activities of the representative(s) or principal(s) are discussed." Often, member firms will hold several group meetings based on functional roles and discuss compliance matters and regulatory updates specific to each of these functional roles. The requirement of an annual meeting ensures that registered representatives and principals remain up to date and educated on compliance matters and are given a forum to voice questions or concerns they may have. It is a chance to step back from the day-to-day functions of the regular business to discuss and consider how effective they have been in operating in a compliant manner and areas of potential improvement.

Principal's Review of a Registered Representative's Written Correspondence

NASD Rule 3010 requires that member firms establish procedures to determine the level of review required and the specific items that must be reviewed by a registered principal prior to distribution. More broadly speaking, the rule states that registered principals must review, endorse, and document in writing all transactions and incoming and outgoing written and electronic correspondence with the public relating to the securities and investment banking business. Additional activities mentioned in the rule that require approval by a registered principal include identifying and handling customer complaints and the proper handling of customers' funds in accordance with the member firm's written procedures. In certain instances where registered principal approval of the previously mentioned activities is not appropriate for the size, business, or structure of such member firm, the firm must train all associated persons to a greater extent than typically required and must provide documentation and surveillance to ensure that procedures are being followed.

Correspondence of Registered Representatives

NASD Rule 3010 provides specific guidance with respect to the recordkeeping and retention requirements for any correspondence from registered representatives. For purposes of this rule, correspondence is defined to mean "any written (including electronic) communication that is distributed or made available to 25 or fewer retail investors within any 30 calendar-day period." The recordkeeping requirements for correspondence require the member firm to retain any correspondence related to its investment banking and securities business along with the names of any persons who prepared or reviewed this correspondence. Also, these listings of names must be readily available and provided for review upon request. The member firm must ensure that this correspondence is retained for a period of at least six years.

Office of Supervisory Jurisdiction and Branch Office

NASD Rule 3010 defines an office of supervisory jurisdiction, or OSJ, as "any office of a member at which any one or more of the following functions take place:

- Order execution and/or market making
- Structuring of public offerings or private placements
- Maintaining custody of customers' funds and/or securities
- Final acceptance (approval) of new accounts on behalf of the member

- Review and endorsement of customer orders, pursuant to paragraph (d) above
- Final approval of retail communications for use by persons associated with the member, pursuant to FINRA Rule 2210(b)(1), except for an office that solely conducts final approval of research reports
- Responsibility for supervising the activities of persons associated with the member at one or more other branch offices of the member."

NASD Rule 3010 defines a branch office as "any location where one or more associated persons of a member regularly conducts the business of effecting any transactions in, or inducing or attempting to induce the purchase or sale of any security, or is held out as such."

Internal Inspections for Offices of Supervisory Jurisdiction, Branch Offices, and Non-Branch Offices

Pursuant to NASD Rule 3010 – Supervision, "Each member shall conduct a review, at least annually, of the businesses in which it engages, which review shall be reasonably designed to assist in detecting and preventing violations of, and achieving compliance with, applicable securities laws and regulations, and with applicable NASD rules." During each investigation, member firms should review the activities of each office of supervisory jurisdiction and any branch office that supervises one or more non-branch locations. For branch offices that do not have any supervisory responsibilities for other locations, inspections only need to occur once every three years. However, factors such as the number of associated persons and the nature and complexity of the business may require more frequent inspections. The member's findings and justification must be included as part of the written supervisory procedures. Finally, all non-branch offices must be inspected on a periodic basis, the determination of which is again based on the nature and complexity of the business and the nature and extent of customer interactions.

Documentation of Internal Inspections

Pursuant to NASD Rule 3010 – Supervision, the topics that must be covered in the written report of an internal investigation include safeguarding of customer funds and securities, maintaining books and records, supervision of customer accounts serviced by branch office managers, transmittal of funds between customers and registered representatives and between customers and third parties, validation of customer address changes, and validation of changes in customer account information. Additionally, the written report must include the dates of inspection of all locations and the frequency and justification of the frequency for inspections of non-supervisory branch offices and non-branch locations. In certain instances, the member may be required to conduct a "heightened inspection" when the person conducting the inspection reports to the branch office manager's supervisor or if the person works in an office supervised by the branch manager's supervisor and the branch office manager generates more than 20 percent of the revenue attributable to the business units under the supervision of the branch manager's supervisor over the prior rolling 12 months. The heightened inspection is meant to avoid conflicts of interest that would undermine the efficacy of the inspection.

Restrictions Surrounding Who Is Permitted to Conduct Internal Inspections

NASD Rule 3010 stipulates specific restrictions surrounding who is permitted to conduct internal inspections in order to mitigate any conflicts of interest and to ensure that inspections are effective in identifying and preventing any violations of securities laws and regulations. Pursuant to the rule, inspections cannot be conducted by a branch office manager, by any person within the office with supervisory responsibilities, or by any person who is supervised by such persons. The exception to this rule is in the case of a member with limited size and resources – such as the case of a single-person office that reports directly to an office of supervisory jurisdiction. In these instances, the member may choose to have a principal conduct the inspection so long as the principal has the knowledge to effectively conduct the inspection. Additionally, the member must document its justification for conducting the inspection in this manner.

Written Customer Complaints

According to FINRA Rule 4513 – Records of Written Customer Complaints – a customer complaint refers to any grievance by a customer or any person authorized to act on behalf of the customer involving the activities of the member or a person associated with the member in connection with the solicitation or execution of any transactions or the disposition of securities or funds of that customer. The clarification of what exactly constitutes a customer complaint is an important distinction because of the recordkeeping and retention requirements with respect to such complaints as well as the impact such complaints have on the long-term record of registered representatives and principals.

According to FINRA Rule 4513 – Records of Written Customer Complaints – each member is required to maintain for a period of at least four years copies of all such written customer complaints relating to that office and any actions taken by the member in response, including all related correspondence. Members have the option to, instead of keeping records at the office of supervisory jurisdiction, make records promptly available at FINRA's request in such locations. By requiring member firms to keep this information readily accessible for several years, it allows for easier access to the written records of these events in the case of further legal action, criminal proceedings, or investigations of member firms or associated persons.

FINRA Rule 4513 – Records of Written Customer Complaints – provides important protections to member firms, registered representatives and principals, and customers. For customers, the rule ensures that the member firm and representative must take the appropriate action with respect to any written complaints they submit and also that these records will be maintained for a period of several years – plenty of time to ensure that the dispute has been resolved. Additionally, the rule protects member firms and registered representatives, both through the documentation of the complaint and the specific guidance around what constitutes a complaint. For instance, not every disagreement between a customer and registered representative will constitute a complaint, and there is often an opportunity to work out any disagreements before the complaint goes on the permanent record of the registered representative.

Process by Which the Public Can Access a Copy of the FINRA Manual

One of the most important aspects of a customer's relationship with member firms and their associated persons is transparency. FINRA Rule 8110 seeks to further that transparency by ensuring that all customers have access to the complete FINRA Manual, which contains all of the rules and provisions that govern the activities of member firms and associated persons. Specifically, the rule provides that members have an obligation to provide access to the FINRA Manual to customers upon request. One of the simplest ways for member firms to meet this obligation is to maintain electronic access to the manual and to provide customers with electronic access to the manual upon request.

FINRA Rule 8210

Role and Rights of an Adjudicator During a FINRA Investigation

Under FINRA Rule 8210, which governs the provision of information and testimony for FINRA investigations, an Adjudicator or FINRA staff shall have the right to:

- Require a member, person associated with a member, or any other person subject to FINRA's jurisdiction to provide information orally, in writing, or electronically (if the requested information is, or is required to be, maintained in electronic form), and to testify at a location specified by FINRA staff, under oath or affirmation administered by a court reporter or a notary public if requested, with respect to any matter involved in the investigation, complaint, examination, or proceeding
- Inspect and copy the books, records, and accounts of such member or person with respect to any matter involved in the investigation, complaint, examination, or proceeding that is in such member's or person's possession, custody, or control.

The granting of this authority to the Adjudicator or FINRA staff is critically important to ensuring that FINRA and other regulatory bodies will have access to records in order to complete a comprehensive investigation.

Conditions Under Which FINRA May Cooperate with Another Domestic or Foreign Regulator or Entity During an Investigation

In the course of an investigation, FINRA staff may need to enter into an information-sharing agreement with a domestic federal agency or foreign regulator. FINRA staff is permitted to enter into such agreements provided the following criteria are met:

- The agency or regulator must agree to treat any shared information confidentially, including not sharing such information upon third-party requests.
- The agency or regulator must have jurisdiction over common regulatory matters at the heart of the investigation.
- The agency or regulator must reciprocate and share information with FINRA as requested.

In addition to investigations, these types of information-sharing agreements can also be entered into for the purpose of market surveillance, enforcement, or other regulatory purposes.

Method by Which Notification of an Investigation Has Been Received

In order to notify a member or firm that it is the subject of an investigation, complaint, or examination, FINRA Rule 8210 provides that the notice will be mailed or otherwise transmitted to the last known business address of the member or the last known residential address of the associated person. The addresses used shall be provided by the Central Registration Depository. However, if the Adjudicator or FINRA staff knows the address in the Central Registration Depository is incorrect, then the notice must be mailed or otherwise transmitted to both the address in the Central Registration Depository and the more current known business address for a member or residential address for an associated person. The notice is considered to have been received once it is sent to these addresses.

Information Submitted Electronically During an Investigation

FINRA Rule 8210 provides that any information submitted electronically to FINRA on a portable media device (flash drive, CD-ROM, DVD, portable hard drive, laptop, computer, disc, etc.) must be encrypted. In order to be properly encrypted under the rule, the portable media device must not be accessible without the use of a confidential process or key. Additionally, the encryption method used must meet minimum industry standards for strong encryption and also provide the confidential process or key needed to access the encrypted information to FINRA in a communication separate from that which contained the encrypted information. These requirements are vital to protecting the confidentiality of any such information that is gathered in the investigative or enforcement process.

Process by Which Trade Information Is Submitted to FINRA for Inspection

FINRA Rules 8211 and 8213 provide the standards for automated submission of trading data that is requested by FINRA during an investigation. For any FINRA requests of an account in which a member or person associated with a member has an interest, the member must submit the clearinghouse numbers for the members on both sides of the transaction, the trading symbol, transaction date, number of shares or quantity of transaction, price, account number, and market center in which the trade was executed. If the transaction involved a customer's account, the member must submit all of the above information and also the customer's name, address, branch, whether the trade was solicited, the opening date of the account, employer, and tax identification number.

Various Sanctions That FINRA Can Impose on a Member Firm

FINRA Rule 8310 allows FINRA to impose a number of sanctions on firms that have violated the securities laws, rules, or regulations, or that have failed to comply with any decisions or orders. Such sanctions include the censure of a member or associated person, levying a fine against a member or associated person, suspending the membership of a member or the registration of an associated person for either a defined period of time or a period contingent on performance of a particular act, expulsion of a member or cancellation of membership or registration of an associated person, suspension of a member or associated person from association with members, imposition of a cease and desist order against a member or associated person, or any other fitting sanction. This rule gives FINRA relatively broad power to impose sanctions as it sees fit for given violations and the particulars of any specific case.

Information That Will and Will Not Be Released Upon an Inquiry Through FINRA BrokerCheck

FINRA BrokerCheck is an online database that provides background and qualification information about brokerage firms, brokers, investment adviser firms, and representatives. Information regarding brokerage firms and brokers comes from the Central Registration Depository (CRD), which is the securities industry online registration and licensing database. Information regarding investment adviser firms and representatives comes from the SEC's Investment Adviser Public Disclosure (IAPD) database. Investors can request an unlimited number of BrokerCheck reports and the requests are not disclosed to the brokers, representatives, or associated firms. These checks will provide physical location and contact information, registration statuses, employment history for the prior 10 years, qualifying examinations that have been passed, and a history of any complaints or arbitrations. Certain information collected during the registration process is not made publicly available, such as Social Security numbers, residential addresses, and any potentially sensitive information contained in any cases that outweigh investor protection concerns.

Disputing the Accuracy of Information Disclosed in That Party's BrokerCheck Report

Under FINRA Rule 8312, there is a three-step process that one must undergo to dispute the accuracy of information contained in BrokerCheck. First, the dispute must be initiated by either a current BrokerCheck firm, any former BrokerCheck firm, or any associated person of a BrokerCheck firm. To initiate the dispute, one of the aforementioned parties must submit a written notice to FINRA clearly identifying the information believed to be inaccurate. FINRA will begin from a place of assuming that the facts and circumstances warrant an investigation into the inaccurate information. However, if the facts and circumstances dictate otherwise, no action will be taken. A note is added to the BrokerCheck record during the process stating that the broker involved has disputed the information in the report. If FINRA determines there are enough facts to confirm the information is correct, then it will be updated in the individual's record.

Releasing Disciplinary Complaints, Decisions, or Other Information from Investigations

Under FINRA Rule 8313, FINRA is obligated to release to the public a copy of any disciplinary complaints or decisions under Rules 9520, 9800, 9552 through 9559, 1015, and 1016. FINRA also maintains the right to release to the public copies of decisions or notices under Rules 6490, 9600, and 9700. The FINRA CEO may also determine additional circumstances in which complaints, decisions, orders, or notifications may be released to the public. These releases must include a notice that the disciplinary complaints only serve to notify the recipient that a formal proceeding has been initiated, but that no findings with respect to the proceeding have been finalized. FINRA also reserves the right to redact certain confidential customer information or waive publication of the document due to investor protection concerns.

Additional Measures Taken If a Fine Is Not Paid in a Timely Manner

Fines and other monetary sanctions can be levied for a number of violations. When these fines are not paid, FINRA Rule 8320 stipulates the options that are available to plan sponsors. First, if the person in question has had a fine levied against her and has not paid within seven days, this rule provides that FINRA may summarily suspend her. FINRA may also choose to summarily revoke the registration of a person of a member who failed to comply. FINRA Rule 8330 further goes on to clarify that the member or person associated with the disciplined member will need to bear all such costs during the proceeding.

Code of Procedure

FINRA Rule 9000 is known as the Code of Procedure and outlines a variety of procedures for handling disciplinary matters for members and associated persons, the regulation of members undergoing financial or operational difficulties, and relief from eligibility requirements of the FINRA By-Laws and rules. More specifically, the 9000 series of rules specifies how and when members and associated persons can be served with complaints or other notices, rules governing appearances related to those complaints or notices, the specific processes and rules for disciplinary proceedings, rules around the extension of time in proceedings, criteria for selection of the panelists in proceedings, the national review procedures of disciplinary proceedings, and conditions for expedited proceedings.

Serving Orders, Notices, Complaints, and Other Papers

FINRA Rule 9134 stipulates that orders, notices, complaints, and other papers may be served on interested parties by either personal service, service by mail by the US postal service, or by courier. Personal service may be accomplished by either handing the papers to the person being served, leaving the papers at the person's office with an employee in charge, or leaving the papers at the person's home with a person "of suitable age and discretion then residing therein." Service by US postal service can be accomplished by sending the papers through first-class mail, first-class certified mail, first-class registered mail, or express mail. The exception is that complaints shall only be served by first-class certified mail or express mail. Service by courier must include a written confirmation of receipt or attempt at delivery.

FINRA Rule 9134 sets forth different rules for the process of serving papers on a natural person compared to an entity. Papers served on natural persons may be served at either the residential address or business address on file in the Central Registration Depository (CRD). If it is known that the address in the CRD is out of date, then duplicate copies can also be served at the person's last known residential address and business address. Papers can also be served on the counsel or representative of a natural person, unless the papers are a complaint or a document initiating a proceeding. Papers served on an entity must be delivered to an officer, partner of a partnership, managing or general agent, or any other agent authorized to accept service. As with a natural person, the papers should be served at the address on file in the CRD. Also, as with a natural person, any papers other than a complaint or document initiating a proceeding can be served on the counsel or a representative.

FINRA Rule 9211

FINRA Rule 9211 has three basic tenets, as follows:

- First, the Department of Enforcement and Department of Market Regulation may request authorization from the Office of Disciplinary Affairs to issue a complaint if they believe that any FINRA member or associated person has violated any rule, regulation, or statutory provision.
- Second, the FINRA Regulation Board and FINRA Board can direct the Office of Disciplinary Affairs to authorize the Department of Enforcement and Department of Market Regulation to issue a complaint when FINRA has jurisdiction over the actions that violated any rule, regulation, or statutory provision.
- Finally, Rule 9211 stipulates that a disciplinary proceeding begins at the point at which the complaint is served and filed.

Circumstances Under Which a Chief Hearing Officer May Consider Ordering a Consolidation of Disciplinary Proceedings

Under FINRA Rule 9214, the Chief Hearing Officer shall take into consideration three factors when determining whether to consolidate disciplinary proceedings with the goal of increasing the efficiency of the disciplinary process and where the complaints involve common questions of law or fact or one or more of the same respondents. The factors to be considered include:

- Whether the same evidence would be presented at each hearing
- Whether the consolidation would benefit the parties to the proceeding through conservation of time and resources
- Whether the consolidation would result in unfair prejudice to any of the parties.

Each of these considerations serves the purpose of maintaining the fairness of the proceedings while most effectively using the time and resources of all parties involved.

Required Response to a Complaint

As provided in FINRA Rule 9215, each respondent to a complaint must serve an answer on all other involved parties within 25 days of the complaint being served. The Hearing Officer has the authority to extend the time beyond 25 days with good cause and must promptly send written notice of receipt of the answer to all parties. The answer that is submitted must specifically admit, deny, or state that the respondent does not have sufficient information to admit or deny each of the complaint's allegations. The respondent may admit or deny only part of an allegation. Any lack of response to an allegation is considered to be admitted. A respondent can also answer with a motion for a more definite statement of specified matters of fact or law, along with the reasoning behind the request for more definite information. If the respondent fails to answer within the specified time, a second notice will be sent and the respondent will have 14 days to reply. If the respondent has still not replied at the end of 14 days, the Hearing Officer may issue a default decision.

Process Whereby a Respondent Can Appeal to the National Adjudicatory Council

Under FINRA Rule 9311, a respondent who has been served a notice of decision under Rule 9268 or 9269 has 25 days to appeal the decision to the National Adjudicatory Council. The appeal will have the effect of staying the decision; however, any permanent cease and desist orders will not be stayed by the appeal. The appeal must be filed with the Office of Hearing Officers and be served on the parties. The appeal must include the name of the disciplinary proceeding, the disciplinary proceeding docket number, the name of the party on whose behalf the appeal is made, a statement of whether oral argument before the National Adjudicatory Council is requested, and a brief statement of findings, conclusions, or sanctions that are being specifically contested.

Authority of the Counsel to the National Adjudicatory Council

FINRA Rule 9313 provides the National Adjudicatory Council with certain authority to more efficiently conduct proceedings, as follows:

- Direct the Office of Hearing Officers to complete and transmit records of disciplinary proceedings to the National Adjudicatory Council
- Establish or amend, but not shorten, a briefing schedule
- Allow deviations of briefs and other documents from the Rule 9310 requirements
- Establish the date, time, and locations of oral arguments and provide for notice of hearings
- Determine who may attend a hearing, other than parties or counsel
- Rule on motions to lengthen or shorten the period of time for the filing of papers
- Create and maintain an official record of the disciplinary proceeding on appeal or review
- Establish the number of copies of papers to be filed with the Adjudicator.

Limitations on the Information to Be Considered in the Review of an Appeal

FINRA Rule 9524 provides more specific guidance on what information is to be considered by the National Adjudicatory Council during the appeal process. As a part of that appeal process, the rule specifically notes that only evidence admitted during the hearing shall be part of the record. Any other evidence that is proffered but not admitted will be retained by the custodian until the date FINRA's decision becomes final or the review is completed. The only information to be considered in the review is the notice originally issued, the documents relied upon in issuing the notice, the application for relief (appeal), any other submissions by the qualified member, any evidence considered at the hearing, and the transcript of the hearing.

Request for Exemptive Relief

A member that is seeking exemptive relief is required to file a written application with the appropriate department of FINRA. The application for exemptive relief must include the applicant's name and address, the name of a person associated with the member who will serve as the primary contact for the application, the Rule from which the member is seeking the exemptive relief, and a statement specifying the reason that exemptive relief should be granted. Applications for exemptive relief will be publicly available as standard practice. If the applicant wants the application to be treated as confidential, the applicant must also include a detailed statement specifying the reason for such request.

Uniform Code of Arbitration

The FINRA Uniform Code of Arbitration, codified in FINRA Rule 10000, provides the guidelines under which disputes between members and other members or persons associated with members must be resolved. These guidelines include the matters that must be brought to arbitration, the composition of various panels and supervision of the arbitration process, the fees paid to arbiters and associated with arbitration proceedings, and the legal ramifications of taking matters to arbitration. The purpose of the Uniform Code of Arbitration is to provide an efficient and cost-effective method for settling intra-industry disputes. The code sets out a specific set of procedures to be followed that are tailored to these matters, as opposed to the legal system that is designed to handle a much wider range of criminal and civil matters. Arbitration also provides for rulings by experienced industry experts who have vast knowledge of the matters in question.

Code of Arbitration Procedure

The administrative provisions under FINRA's Code of Arbitration Procedure, as codified in FINRA Rule 10100, provide specific guidance as to the application of the Code. More specifically, the administrative provisions outline the circumstances under which a member can be deemed to have failed to act properly under the Code, the types of matters that can be submitted for arbitration, the purpose and responsibilities of the National Arbitration and Mediation Committee, the responsibilities of the Director of Arbitration, and the fees, known as honorarium, paid to arbitrators. Additionally, the administrative provisions contain clauses stating that one party in an arbitration may not initiate legal action against any of the other parties involved in the arbitration during that time, and finally that matters within arbitration proceedings are still subject to disciplinary review and action by FINRA.

Mediation Rules

Under FINRA Rule 14000, any matter that is submitted for arbitration can be settled through mediation, but only if all parties agree. The parties to a mediation have the option to determine whether they will represent themselves, be represented by an attorney, or be represented by some other external third party. The mediator used in proceedings may either be selected if agreed to by the parties to the mediation or, if an agreement cannot be reached, by the Director of Mediation. The benefits to utilizing mediation are numerous, including lower costs, more flexible proceedings, and the ability to reach a mutually agreed-upon resolution in the form of a compromise between the parties.

Insider Trading and Securities Fraud Enforcement Act of 1988

The Insider Trading and Securities Fraud Enforcement Act of 1988 is designed to protect investors and the public interest by specifying the rules and enforcement of penalties around trading securities while in the possession of material, nonpublic information about those securities. The Act requires brokers, dealers, and investment advisers to "establish, maintain and enforce written policies and procedures...to prevent the misuse" of material, nonpublic information. If found to be in violation of insider trading laws, one is liable to any other investors who had transacted in the same class of the same security contemporaneously. The maximum penalties imposed by the Act were raised to a fine of $1 million and 10 years in prison.

Civil and Criminal Penalties That Can Be Imposed by the SEC Against Violators of Insider Trading Laws

The Insider Trading and Securities Fraud Enforcement Act of 1988 imposed new and more stringent civil and criminal penalties for those who have violated insider trading laws. Under the Act, the SEC was granted the authority to impose damages for three times the amount of profit gained or loss avoided in the illegal transactions up to a maximum of $1,000,000. The criminal penalties for violating insider trading laws were made more stringent by the Act. The maximum fines were increased from $100,000 to $1,000,000 for individuals and from $500,000 to $2,500,000 for non-natural persons. Additionally, the maximum jail sentence was increased from five years to 10 years. Finally, the Act provides that all non-natural persons are subject to the higher fines under the criminal penalties as compared to the civil penalties.

Civil Penalties

Under the Insider Trading and Securities Fraud Enforcement Act of 1988, the SEC has the authority to bring a civil action against a person who has violated the act or the person who controlled the person who committed the act. In order to authorize the civil penalty or action, the SEC will bring an action to a United States District Court, which is granted the authority to determine whether a penalty will be imposed and the amount of the penalty, subject to certain limits. The maximum civil penalty for the person who committed the violation is limited to three times the amount of profit gained or loss avoided as a result of the illegal activity, and the penalty for a controlling person is limited to the greater of $1 million or three times the amount of profit gained or loss avoided.

The Insider Trading and Securities Fraud Enforcement Act of 1988 and the Securities Exchange Act of 1934 provide that contemporaneous traders, those who traded in the same class of security contemporaneously with the insider trader and who were affected by the insider trading, have a right of action against the insider trader. Action must be brought within the time frame for the statute of limitations, which is five years in this case. The liability of the insider trader to the contemporaneous trader is limited to the amount of loss that resulted from the insider trading. Non-contemporaneous traders may also be able to bring action against the insider trader in certain circumstances, such as when the insider trading action affected the sale price of the firm. However, the laws and regulations are vaguer with these non-contemporaneous traders.

Preventing the Misuse of Material, Non-Public Information

Employee training, employee trading restrictions, and physical barriers are all critical components in reducing the potential for misuse of material, non-public information. Employee training is important so that all employees understand what constitutes material, non-public information. Additionally, all employees need to know what steps they should take if they come across such information and also what actions to avoid so that they do not take any illegal action based on such information. Employee trading restrictions, such as the use of watch lists for companies currently doing business with the firm or restricted lists where the company is aware of the heightened potential for acquiring material, non-public information, aid employees in identifying certain securities or timing of transactions to avoid and aid compliance departments in flagging potentially problematic transactions. Finally, physical barriers between departments, such as investment banking and research teams, can help to minimize the risk of an incidental transfer of material, non-public information through overheard conversations or reports left on a printer.

Interdepartmental Barriers

In order to prevent the incidental transfer and potential misuse of material, non-public information within a firm, many companies will establish physical barriers between departments that are especially susceptible to such transfer. For instance, the research department of a firm may be able to benefit greatly from information gathered by that same firm's investment banking and underwriting teams. Without physical barriers, it is very likely that employees could accidentally overhear conversations or pick up the wrong email or presentation off of a printer. Worse yet, less honest employees would have access to information they feel could give them a competitive advantage and may be willing to violate the laws to do so. To combat these accidental and intentional violations, companies may establish separate office spaces for these types of departments that are frequently exposed to sensitive information and will frequently also establish additional security measures.

Review Procedures

Firms should take a number of measures to both prevent and monitor the potential misuse of material, non-public information. Some examples of policies and procedures designed to prevent the misuse of material, non-public information include physical barriers between certain departments within a company, implementation of blackout policies and trading windows for certain individuals at certain times, and required pre-clearance of trades in certain circumstances. Companies are able to monitor employees' acquisition and use of material, non-public information by receiving duplicate copies of all brokerage accounts for registered representatives. Additionally, firms may monitor any electronic communications and can encourage the reporting of material, non-public information through the firm's compliance department to ensure no one else is utilizing this information.

Fidelity Bonds

FINRA Rule 4360 specifies certain minimum types and amounts of blanket fidelity bond coverages that members must maintain to be permitted to join the Securities Investor Protection Corporation (SIPC). The member must, at a minimum, maintain coverage for (i) Fidelity, (ii) On Premises, (iii) In Transit, (iv) Forgery and Alteration, (v) Securities, and (vi) Counterfeit Currency. The member's fidelity bond must provide coverage on a per-loss basis without an aggregate liability limit and must meet the minimum coverage requirements, which are determined based on the member's required net capital under SEA Rule 15c3-1. The minimum coverages range from $600,000 for members with a net capital requirement of $250,000-300,000, all the way to $5 million for members with a net capital requirement of greater than $12 million. Members with net capital requirements under $250,000 must maintain minimum coverage equal to the greater of 120 percent of the required net capital or $100,000.

Periodic Review of the Fidelity Bond Coverage

FINRA Rule 4360 specifies certain minimum types and amounts of blanket fidelity bond coverage that members must maintain to be permitted to join the Securities Investor Protection Corporation (SIPC). In addition, Rule 4360 also specifies requirements with respect to review of these coverages. To ensure that FINRA is notified in the event of any changes or cancellations of coverage, one requirement is that each policy include a cancellation rider that notifies FINRA if the coverage is cancelled or substantially modified. Additionally, members must review their coverage at least annually to ensure its adequacy. The minimum coverage requirements are based on the member's highest net capital requirement during the preceding 12-month period. Newer members must also ensure that they carry as much coverage in their second year as they had in their first, regardless of what the aforementioned testing would specify as the requirement.

Available Exemptions

FINRA Rule 4360 specifies certain minimum types and amounts of blanket fidelity bond coverage that members must maintain to be permitted to join the Securities Investor Protection Corporation (SIPC). Additionally, Rule 4360 provides important exemptions from these requirements under certain limited circumstances. For instance, members that maintain a security bond in connection with their registration on a national securities exchange that is registered with the SEC may apply for exemption if the member is in good standing with the exchange and the fidelity bond requirements of the exchange are at least equal to the requirements under this rule. Certain other members that do not conduct business directly with the public are also exempt from the requirements of this rule, including designated market makers, floor brokers, and registered floor traders. Finally, certain other members may apply for an exemption based on substantial changes in the member's business that would result in a lower net capital requirement.

FINRA Rule 3270

FINRA Rule 3270 – Outside Business Activities of Registered Persons – restricts registered persons from being compensated, or having a reasonable expectation of being compensated, for activities outside their relationship with their member firm without having provided the required prior written notice to the member firm. The required form of this prior written notice is determined by each member firm. Registered persons represent their member firms in all that they do, and member firms are responsible for the actions of their registered persons. That responsibility includes knowledge and supervision of any ways in which that registered representative is engaging in business practices and being compensated. Failure to know about or supervise a registered person outside business activities could result in significant consequences, both for the registered person and for the member firm.

Outside Business Activity That Would Not Be Permitted

FINRA Rule 3270 – Outside Business Activities of Registered Persons – restricts registered persons from being compensated, or having a reasonable expectation of being compensated, for activities outside their relationship with their member firm without having provided the required prior written notice to the member firm. One example of an outside business activity that would be prohibited is the publishing of a paid, online investment newsletter that individuals can choose to subscribe to and pay a fee to the registered person. This activity would not only divide the registered person's time and attention from his duties to his member firm, but could also present a conflict of interest between the member firm's opinions and research and the recommendations that the registered person is making to his subscribers. Finally, without knowledge of this activity, the member firm has no means of supervising the registered person's activities.

Outside Business Activity That a Registered Representative Could Engage in Without Creating a Conflict of Interest

FINRA Rule 3270 – Outside Business Activities of Registered Persons – restricts registered persons from being compensated, or having a reasonable expectation of being compensated, for activities outside their relationship with their member firm without having provided the required prior written notice to the member firm. A registered person could engage in an outside business activity preparing test preparation materials for another company not related to his member firm without creating a conflict of interest, despite being paid for his work. The registered person may be required to disclose the time spent on the outside business activity and any compensation earned, but as long as the work does not pose a conflict with his member firm's business, this activity may be permitted with prior written notice and approval.

NASD Rule 3040

NASD Rule 3040 sets forth the requirements for any person associated with a member firm to participate in a private securities transaction. Prior to participating in a private securities transaction, a person associated with a member firm must provide written notice to the member firm, including a detailed description of the private securities transaction, information about the associated person's role in the transaction, and whether or not the associated person has or will receive any type of selling compensation as a result of the transaction. If the private securities transaction comprises a series of related transactions with no selling compensation involved, the associated person is permitted to provide only a single written notice for the entire series of related transactions.

Private Securities Transaction and Selling Compensation

NASD Rule 3040 sets forth the requirements for any person associated with a member firm to participate in a private securities transaction. Two key terms within this rule are "private securities transaction" and "selling compensation."

The Rule defines a "private securities transaction" as "any securities transaction outside the regular course or scope of an associated person's employment with a member, including, though not limited to, new offerings of securities which are not registered with the Commission." Excluded from this definition are transactions among immediate family members with no selling compensation and personal transactions in investment company and variable annuity securities.

The Rule further defines "selling compensation" as "any compensation paid directly or indirectly from whatever source in connection with or as a result of the purchase or sale of a security, including, but not limited to, commissions; finder's fees; securities or rights to acquire securities; rights of participation in profits, tax benefits or dissolution proceeds, as a general partner or otherwise; or expense reimbursements."

Notice and Approval Between a Private Securities Transaction for Compensation and Not for Compensation

NASD Rule 3040 specifies that a person associated with a member firm must provide written notice to the member firm prior to engaging in a private securities transaction, whether or not the associated person will be receiving selling compensation. However, there are differences in the approval process of the member firm depending on whether or not the associated person is receiving selling compensation. In private securities transactions in which the associated person is receiving selling compensation, the member firm must reply in writing to the associated person indicating whether it approves or disapproves of the associated person's participation in the proposed transaction. If approved, the member firm records the transaction on its books and records, and supervises the activities of the associated person. If disapproved, the associated person is strictly prohibited from participating in the transaction in any manner. If the associated person is not receiving selling compensation, the member firm does not have to provide approval or disapproval, but may specify the conditions under which the associated person may participate in the transaction.

NASD Rule 3050

NASD Rule 3050 requires that a member that executes a securities transaction for the account of a person associated with another member must use reasonable due diligence to determine that the transaction will not adversely affect the interests of the employer member of the associated person. The rule also applies to transactions for any accounts over which the associated person has discretionary authority. Obligations for the executing member, associated persons who have accounts with members, and associated persons who have accounts with investment advisers or banks are further clarified. Transactions in investment company shares and unit investments trusts or accounts that are limited to such securities are exempt from the requirements of this rule.

Requirements of an Executing Member When That Member Knows That a Person Associated with an Employer Member Has a Financial Interest in or Discretionary Authority over an Account Carried by the Executing Member

NASD Rule 3050 sets forth three requirements for an executing member when that member knows that a person associated with an employer member will have a financial interest in or discretionary authority over an account carried by the executing member. First, the executing member is required to notify the employer member of the associated person, in writing and prior to the execution of any transactions in the account, of the person's intention to open such account. Next, the executing member is required, if requested in writing, to provide duplicate copies of confirmations, statements, or other account-related information. Finally, the executing member is required to notify the associated person that the information above will be provided to the employer member.

Obligations of Associated Persons Concerning an Account with a Member

NASD Rule 3050 provides that a person associated with a member must notify both the employer member and executing member, in writing and prior to opening the account or placing the initial order for the purchase or sale of securities, of the person's association and activity with the other member. The rule applies not only to accounts established after the person's association with the member, but also to accounts in existence upon the person's association with that member or a new member. In those circumstances, the associated person must provide notification to both members upon becoming associated with the member. These obligations, in conjunction with the executing member's notification obligations, provide some duplication but help to ensure no accounts go without notification.

Obligations Imposed on Associated Persons Concerning an Account with an Investment Adviser, Bank, or Other Financial Institution

NASD Rule 3050 sets forth two requirements for persons associated with a member who open securities accounts or place an order for the purchase or sale of securities with a notice-registered broker-dealer, investment adviser, bank, or other financial institution. First, the associated person must notify his employer member in writing and prior to the execution of any transactions of his intent to open the account. Additionally, the associated person must, if requested in writing by his employer member, request in writing and ensure that the entity with which he executes the transactions or maintains the account provides duplicate copies of confirmations, account statements, or other account information, as requested. This rule applies both to accounts opened before and after an associated person becomes so associated, and compliance with the rule is required upon the later of opening the account or becoming an associated person.

FINRA Rule 3220

FINRA Rule 3220 – Influencing or Rewarding Employees of Others – prohibits members and persons associated with members from giving anything of value greater than $100 per individual per year to any person where such payment is in relation to the business of the employer of the recipient. The rule also applies to gratuities, including gifts. Recipients covered under this rule include any person, principal, proprietor, employee agent, or representative where the exchange is in relation to the business of that individual's employer. This rule is meant to prohibit members or associated persons from trying to exert influence over the decisions of their business partners through lavish gifts.

FINRA Rule 3220 – Influencing or Rewarding Employees of Others – prohibits members and persons associated with members from giving anything of value greater than $100 per individual per year to any person where such payment is in relation to the business of the employer of the recipient. It is important for members and associated persons to understand the circumstances under which these limitations do not apply. For instance, the rule states that these limitations do not apply to contracts of employment with or compensation for services rendered by those persons as long as there is a written agreement prior to the performance of services outlining the nature of the employment, the amount of compensation, and the written consent of each person's employer or principal.

FINRA Rule 4530

Due to the significant overlap between the disclosure requirements of FINRA Rule 4530 and the reporting requirements under Forms U4, U5, and BD, FINRA has provided some accommodations to eliminate duplication of efforts in reporting this information. For instance, the reporting requirements under Rule 4530 Section (a)(1) need not be met if the member discloses such event in accordance with the terms of Form U4 and indicates that such disclosure covers the reporting requirements under this rule. Additionally, certain reporting requirements under paragraphs (a) and (b) of Rule 4530 can be met by reporting those same events on Form U5. However, not all of the reporting requirements are consistent. One example is the reporting of a criminal indictment, criminal complaint, or plea agreement, which must meet a certain dollar threshold for reporting on Form U4 but is not subject to such thresholds to be reportable under Rule 4530.

FINRA Rule 4530 specifies a number of events that member firms and associated persons are required to report and the time frames in which they must be reported. Certain notable events must be reported promptly to FINRA, including:

- Indictments, criminal complaints, or plea agreements
- Complaints in which the member is named as a defendant in any securities- or commodities-related private civil litigation
- Any securities- or commodities-related arbitration claim or financial-related insurance arbitration claim filed against a member
- Any violation reportable under question 14 on Form U4 for a person associated with the member.

Other events must be reported no later than 30 days, including when the member or an associated person:

- Has violated any securities-, insurance-, commodities-, financial-, or investment-related laws or regulations of any regulatory bodies or professional organizations
- Is the subject of a customer complaint involving theft or misappropriation of funds or forgery
- Is named as a defendant in a proceeding brought by a regulatory body or self-regulatory organization
- Is denied registration, suspended, or disciplined by any regulatory body or self-regulatory organization
- Is indicted or convicted of any felony or misdemeanor that relates to a securities transaction, bribery, perjury, theft, embezzlement, or a number of other similar crimes
- Holds a leadership position in an organization that is denied registration, suspended, or disciplined by a regulatory body or self-regulatory organization
- Is involved with any person subject to a statutory disqualification.

Reporting Requirements for Customer Complaints

NASD Rule 4530 requires that members provide to FINRA statistical and summary information regarding written customer complaints, subject to the level of detail requested by FINRA, by the fifteenth day of the month following the calendar quarter in which the member received the customer complaints. More specific and individual customer complaint information may be required to be provided on a more frequent and timely basis by FINRA. For example, the member must submit notification to FINRA within 30 days if the written customer complaint included allegations of theft, misappropriation of funds or securities, or forgery. Additionally, the member must report promptly to FINRA if it is the defendant in a complaint that involves securities- or commodities-related private civil litigation.

Use of Information Obtained in a Fiduciary Capacity

FINRA Rule 2060 – Use of Information Obtained in a Fiduciary Capacity – prohibits a member from utilizing information gathered from a client about the ownership of securities to solicit additional purchases, sales, or exchanges except at the request or on behalf of the issuer. A fiduciary is only able to do his job well if the client shares information openly and freely and if the client trusts the fiduciary to be acting in his best interests. By restricting the use of this personal information from solicitation, FINRA is enabling the fiduciary and ensuring clients that their fiduciaries are acting solely in their best interests and not in the best interests of their employer member or business partners.

Larceny and Embezzlement

Section 37 of the Investment Company Act of 1940 – Larceny and Embezzlement – deems it a crime for one to commit larceny or embezzlement and subjects those crimes to punishments detailed in Section 49 of the Act. Larceny is defined in the Act as stealing, unlawfully abstracting, or unlawfully and willfully converting to his own use or the use of another. While these crimes are typically thought to relate to cash and securities, they may also apply to credits, properties, or assets of any investment company. The act clearly defines the types of instruments that can be stolen, misappropriated, or embezzled and also sets forth a clear punishment for those convicted, including a fine of up to $10,000 and up to five years in prison.

Sales Practices

Requirements of Section 10 of the Securities Act of 1933

Prospectus

Section 10 of the Securities Act of 1933 delineates certain requirements for information that must be contained within a prospectus, including all the information contained within the security's registration statement. For domestic securities, the prospectus may exclude the information from paragraphs 28 to 32 of schedule A of the registration statement. For securities issued by foreign governments, the prospectus may exclude the documents from paragraphs 13 and 14 of schedule B of the registration statement. The Commission may also deem other information unnecessary for inclusion in the prospectus if it is not necessary for the protection of investors. Section 10 also specifies that if the prospectus is used more than nine months after the date of the registration statement, then the information contained in the prospectus must not be more than 16 months old.

Summary Prospectus

Under Section 10(b) of the Securities Act of 1933, the Commission may allow for the use of a summary prospectus, which need not contain all of the information contained within the registration statement. This condensed, summary prospectus allows investors to view certain information about the security without digging through the entire prospectus, and will point the investor to where the full prospectus is available for additional information. The summary prospectus is typically filed with the registration statement, and the Commission has the right to suspend or revoke the use of this summary prospectus if it is found to be misleading or contain untrue statements of material fact, or if the Commission determines that such summary prospectus is not in the best interest of the investing public.

Amended Prospectus

Section 10 of the Securities Act of 1933 provides the Commission with the authority to issue an order that would prevent or suspend the use of a summary prospectus. Some examples of situations in which this might occur would be if the Commission felt that the summary prospectus had not been filed or if it included untrue statements of material facts or omissions of any material facts required to make the statements therein not misleading. When a summary prospectus is suspended, the Commission will notify the issuing company, which will have the opportunity for a hearing or will send a telegraphic notice of confirmation. Once the prospectus has been amended or filed, the Commission will lift the order and it can once again be used in accordance with the Act.

Section 12 of the Securities Act of 1933

Civil Liabilities Arising in Connection with Prospectuses and Communications

Section 12 of the Securities Act of 1933 states that any person who either offers or sells a security in violation of Section 5 of the Act (an unregistered security) or offers or sells a security by means of a prospectus or oral communication that includes an untrue statement of material fact or omits to state a material fact that is necessary to make other statements not misleading, even if he could not have known about the untruth or omission with reasonable care, can be held liable to the person purchasing the security from him. The purchaser may sue in any court of competent jurisdiction to recover the amount paid for the security, plus interest thereon, less income received. The purchaser can also sue to recover damages if he no longer owns the security.

Extent to Which a Loss Is Recoverable If a Portion of the Loss Can Be Proven to Not Be Related to an Untrue Statement or Omission of Material Fact in the Prospectus or Other Communication

Section 12 of the Securities Act of 1933 contemplates the civil penalties when any person unknowingly offers or sells a security that is either unregistered or is accompanied by a prospectus or statement that includes an untrue material statement or omission of a necessary material statement. The purchaser may sue to recover the amount paid, plus interest thereon, less income received. However, the person who sold or offered the security may attempt to prove that some or all of the depreciation of the asset or attempted recoverable amount is not related to the portion of the prospectus or statement that was inaccurate or omitted a statement of material fact.

Rule 134

A number of statements can be made concerning a security that do not constitute a prospectus pursuant to Rule 134, provided a registration statement and prospectus have already been filed:

- Factual information about the legal identity and business location of the issuer
- Title of the security and the amount being offered
- Brief indication of the general type of business of the issuer
- The price of the security or the methodology for determining the price
- Final maturity and interest rate provisions for fixed-income securities
- Yield or probable yield range for fixed-income securities with fixed interest rate provisions
- Brief description of the intended use of the proceeds of the offering
- Contact information for the sender of the communication and whether or not it expects to participate in the offering
- Type of underwriting

- Names of the underwriters participating in the offering
- Anticipated schedule for the offering
- Description of the procedures by which underwriters will conduct the offering
- Legal counsel's opinion as to whether the security is a legal investment for savings banks, fiduciaries, and similar investors, and whether it is permissible under ERISA
- Legal counsel's opinion as to exemption from specified taxes
- Statements or legends required by state laws
- Names of security exchanges where it will be listed, ticker symbol, CUSIP.

Certain Statements Can Be Made That Are Not Deemed to Be a Prospectus

Rule 134 provides that certain statements can be made that are not deemed to be a prospectus, so long as the registration statement and prospectus have previously been filed. The statements provided exemption under this rule are limited to statements of indisputable fact such as business locations, business descriptions, offering prices, exchange listings, and ticker symbols and CUSIP numbers, among others. This allows the underwriters and issuers to communicate about the offering, not in the form of solicitation of investment, without constantly having to be concerned about every communication meeting the requirements for prospectuses. These types of exemptions are critical to the efficient functioning of markets, and to impose the prospectus limitations and requirements to these basic types of communications would not serve to protect the investing public in any meaningful way.

Additional Statements That Need to Be Included with the Exempted Statements When the Registration Statement Has Not Yet Become Effective

Rule 134 provides that certain statements can be made that are not deemed to be a prospectus, so long as the registration statement and prospectus have previously been filed. In situations in which the registration statement has not yet been filed, these statements must also include a disclosure that "A registration statement relating to these securities has been filed with the Securities and Exchange Commission but has not yet become effective. These securities may not be sold nor may offers to buy be accepted prior to the time the registration statement becomes effective." It must also include the name or a URL where the prospectus is available. Additionally, the statements may be contained in a communication which is limited to a statement of from whom a written prospectus can be obtained and indicates the security, the price, and who will be executing orders.

Rule 135a

Generic Advertising

Under Rule 135a of the Securities Act of 1933, generic advertising will not be considered as an offering of a security so long as it meets at least one of the following requirements:

- Explanatory information relating to securities of investment companies generally or to the nature of investment companies, or to services offered in connection with the ownership of such securities
- The mention or explanation of investment companies of different generic types or having various investment objectives, such as balanced funds, growth funds, income funds, leveraged funds, specialty funds, variable annuities, bond funds, and no-load funds
- Offers, descriptions, and explanation of various products and services not constituting a security subject to registration under the Act, provided that such offers, descriptions, and explanations do not relate directly to the desirability of owning or purchasing a security issued by a registered investment company
- Invitation to inquire for further information.

Requirements of the Sponsoring Registered Broker or Dealer

Under Rule 135a of the Securities Act of 1933, generic advertising will not be considered as an offering of a security so long as it meets at least one of four requirements. In instances where the communication contains a solicitation of inquiries and prospectuses are to be sent in response to such inquiries, the sponsoring company must indicate the number of such investment companies and a disclosure that the sponsoring company is acting as the principal underwriter or investment adviser. The sponsoring company is also required to include in the communication the name and address of a registered broker-dealer or the sponsoring company so the recipient knows whom to contact for additional information.

Rule 156

Material Facts

Pursuant to Rule 156 of the Securities Act of 1933, there are two requirements related to material facts. The first requirement is that investment company sales literature may not contain an untrue statement of material fact. Additionally, investment company sales literature may not omit to state a material fact that is necessary in order to make a statement made not misleading. Each circumstance is considered within the context in which the statement is made, and will be evaluated in conjunction with other statements made in connection with the sale of the same security and the absence of other explanations or qualifications that are necessary to make a statement not misleading, among others. Potential investors need to be made aware of all material facts related to an investment company security to allow them to make an informed investment decision.

SALES LITERATURE

Rule 156, which governs investment company sales literature and sets forth the circumstances under which sales literature could be considered misleading or misrepresentative, provides for a very specific definition of sales literature, as opposed to generic advertising or communications. "Sales literature" is defined "to include any communication (whether in writing, by radio, or by television) used by any person to offer to sell or induce the sale of securities of any investment company." This definition includes communications between issuers, underwriters, and dealers if the information in those communications can be reasonably expected to be relayed to prospective investors or is meant to be used in the offer or sale of securities.

Rule 156 sets forth two specific criteria that can be used to determine if sales literature is misleading. First, sales literature may be misleading if it contains an untrue statement of material fact. For instance, a fund may identify itself as being a mid-cap growth fund, when in fact the characteristics of its underlying investments have shifted over recent months and would now be considered mid-cap value. Additionally, sales literature could be considered misleading if it omits a material fact that is necessary in order to make the included statements not misleading. For instance, when presenting the fund's investment performance history, it would be misleading to omit to state the material fact that the fund had made a considerable shift in style two years ago. A large portion of the performance history would be attributable to the previous investment style and would not be relevant to the evaluation of the current fund being offered for sale.

REPRESENTATIONS OF PAST OR FUTURE INVESTMENT PERFORMANCE

Rule 156 specifies two broad circumstances under which representations of past or future investment performance could be misleading. First, it could be considered misleading if representations of past performance of either an actual or hypothetical investment convey results that are not justified, could not be achieved, or omit necessary explanations or disclosures. For instance, a historical performance representation that assumes that funds were reallocated at times chosen based on the back-testing model, when such reallocation would have been unlikely at the time it was shown to have occur, would be misleading. Additionally, it would be misleading to make representations about the security of capital, that future performance will reflect prior performance, or that prior gains would predict future gains. One example of this would be in the case of a fixed-income security where the principal amount invested is typically stable and expected to be repaid at a specified, future maturity date. However, it would be misleading to represent that this capital is safe or guaranteed in any way.

STATEMENT INVOLVING A MATERIAL FACT ABOUT THE CHARACTERISTICS OR ATTRIBUTES OF AN INVESTMENT COMPANY

Rule 156 sets forth three specific circumstances under which a statement of material fact could be considered to be misleading. First, a statement within the sales literature could be misleading because of other statements made in connection with the sale of the security, because of the omission of necessary explanations or limitations to make the statement not misleading, or due to general economic or financial conditions. Next, sales literature could be considered misleading because of representations of past or future investment performance. This may include portrayals of past performance by hypothetical investments that are not justified or false representations about security of capital, expenses, or future gains or income. For instance, a security may use back-testing to show its hypothetical performance over a given period of time. If the fact that this back-testing is hypothetical is not properly disclosed, that would be considered misleading. Finally, a statement could be misleading if equal prominence in the discussion is not given to both the possible benefits and the risks or if the statement makes exaggerations or unwarranted comparisons to other investment products. Such an unwarranted comparison and incomplete explanation of risk could occur if a registered person was trying to compare the greater yield from preferred stock to a corporate bond without a discussion of the inherent risks of preferred stock and lower seniority in the corporate debt structure.

Rule 482

In order to comply with Rule 482 of the Securities Act of 1933, any advertisement of an investment company must include a statement that advises an investor to consider the investment objectives, risks, charges, and expenses of the investment company carefully before investing; explains that the prospectus and, if available, the summary prospectus contain this and other information about the investment company; identifies a source from which an investor may obtain a prospectus and, if available, a summary prospectus; and states that the prospectus and, if available, the summary prospectus should be read carefully before investing. This disclosure is important because it ensures that each piece of investment company advertising will remind investors to carefully consider their investments and points them in the right direction to obtain additional information that is necessary to make an informed decision.

Requirements Relating to Performance Data That Are Imposed as It Relates to Advertising by an Investment Company

In order to comply with Rule 482 of the Securities Act of 1933, any investment company advertisements including performance data must include the following:

- A legend disclosing that the performance data quoted represents past performance; that past performance does not guarantee future results; that the investment return and principal value of an investment will fluctuate so that an investor's shares, when redeemed, may be worth more or less than their original cost; and that current performance may be lower or higher than the performance data quoted. The legend should also identify either a toll-free (or collect) telephone number or a website where an investor may obtain performance data current to the most recent month-end unless the advertisement includes total return quotations current to the most recent month ended seven business days prior to the date of use. An advertisement for a money market fund may omit the disclosure about principal value fluctuation; and if a sales load or any other nonrecurring fee is charged, the maximum amount of the load or fee, and if the sales load or fee is not reflected, a statement that the performance data does not reflect the deduction of the sales load or fee, and that, if reflected, the load or fee would reduce the performance quoted.

Restrictions on the Use of Applications in Sales Literature

Rule 482 of the Securities Act of 1933, which governs advertising by investment companies, states that an advertisement that complies with this rule may not contain or be accompanied by an application that can be used by a prospective investor to invest in the investment company. There is a notable exception to this restriction on the inclusion of applications, however. A prospectus of a unit investment trust offering variable annuity or variable life insurance contracts may include an application to invest in the unit investment trust so long as the prospectus includes or is accompanied by such information about the investment company that the unit investment trust is investing in such that it would be deemed a prospectus.

Information That Must Be Included in Any Sales Literature

Rule 34b-1 provides important guidance for investment companies in developing sales literature that accurately portrays their security and would not be classified as misleading to investors. Specifically, sales literature must contain the following:

- A statement that advises an investor to consider the investment objectives, risks, charges, and expenses of the investment company carefully before investing, explains where the investor may obtain the prospectus and statement of additional information, and that the prospectus should be read carefully before investing
- Advertisements used prior to the effectiveness of the registration statement must include a "subject to completion" legend

- Advertisements including performance data must include:
- A legend disclosing that data quoted represents past performance and that past performance does not guarantee future results
- The investment return and principal value of an investment will fluctuate and the value may be worth more or less than the original investment
- A toll-free phone line to obtain the most current performance data as of the most recent month-end
- Maximum loads or fees that could be charged under the product.

Standards of Commercial Honor and Principles of Trade

FINRA Rule 2010 – Standards of Commercial Honor and Principles of Trade – states that "A member, in the conduct of its business, shall observe high standards of commercial honor and just and equitable principles of trade." Broadly speaking, this rule encourages members to be just and equitable in their dealings, although no real specific guidance is provided. This broad, ethical standard is meant to cover all aspects of a registered representative's business, whether that involves dealings with customers, his interactions with his member firm or other member firms, or dealings with FINRA and other regulatory bodies. For instance, registered persons have been found to have violated FINRA Rule 2010 for failing to timely and accurately disclose material items on their Form U4.

An example of a violation of FINRA Rule 2010 – Standards of Commercial Honor and Principles of Trade – would be a member that treats customers differently based on their gender, ethnicity, religion, or other personal attributes. For instance, if a registered person of a member firm was found to have placed trades in accounts for other members of his race or religious background ahead of trades of customers of other backgrounds, then that registered person would be in violation of FINRA Rule 2010, among others. This biased approach to customers violates the just and equitable charge of Rule 2010, as well as a number of other FINRA rules, and would result in significant repercussions for the member. A member must treat each customer equitably, considering each customer's individual circumstances and investment objectives. It is important to the efficient functioning of capital markets, member firms, and registered persons that their customers believe that they are being treated fairly.

Use of Manipulative, Deceptive or Other Fraudulent Devices

FINRA Rule 2020 – Use of Manipulative, Deceptive or Other Fraudulent Devices – states that "No member shall effect any transaction in, or induce the purchase or sale of, any security by means of any manipulative, deceptive or other fraudulent device or contrivance." For instance, members may not make material representations to customers about securities that the member or registered person knows to be inaccurate. Additionally, the member or registered person may not intentionally omit a material fact about the security in recommending that the customer purchase or sell the security. The importance of this rule is in ensuring the integrity of the capital markets and the confidence of retail investors that the markets are not "rigged" for the larger, institutional investors or those with critical inside information.

Example of a Violation

A member or registered person would be in violation of Rule 2020 if it or she used falsified, enhanced financial reports to entice an investor to purchase a certain security. For instance, consider the example of a registered person recommending to a customer the purchase of the equity security of ABC Company. ABC Company has just recently defaulted on a debt obligation. However, in providing the financial reports of ABC Company to the customer, the registered person fails to present this material financial development. The registered person has failed to disclose a material fact about ABC Company. In addition to being dishonest and illegal, such activities have significantly negative repercussions for the markets, as they reduce market efficiency and drastically reduce market participation among smaller investors if discovered.

Communications with the Public

FINRA Rule 2210 provides for the following five general standards for all communications with the public:

- All member communications with the public shall be based on principles of fair dealing and good faith, must be fair and balanced, and must provide a sound basis for evaluating the facts in regard to any particular security or type of security, industry, or service. No member may omit any material fact or qualification if the omission, in the light of the context of the material presented, would cause the communications to be misleading.
- No member may make any false, exaggerated, unwarranted, or misleading statement or claim in any communication with the public. No member may publish, circulate, or distribute any public communication that the member knows or has reason to know contains any untrue statement of a material fact or is otherwise false or misleading.
- Information may be placed in a legend or footnote only in the event that such placement would not inhibit an investor's understanding of the communication.
- Communications with the public may not predict or project performance, imply that past performance will recur, or make any exaggerated or unwarranted claim, opinion, or forecast. A hypothetical illustration of mathematical principles is permitted, provided that it does not predict or project the performance of an investment or investment strategy.
- If any testimonial in a communication with the public concerns a technical aspect of investing, the person making the testimonial must have the knowledge and experience to form a valid opinion.

Example of a Violation

ABC Investment Company places an advertisement in *The Wall Street Journal* regarding its newest XYZ Fund. The advertisement states that based on complex back-testing and algorithms, XYZ Fund can be expected to continue to earn returns in excess of 20 percent per year. Additionally, the advertisement contains a testimonial from Joe Smith, an elementary school teacher who is new to investing, recommending the fund for its ability to minimize downside risk. This advertisement violates FINRA Rule 2210 in two important ways. First, FINRA Rule 2210 prohibits the use of past performance or back-testing to implicate future performance, even if such performance is not guaranteed. Additionally, the testimonial provided concerns a technical aspect, downside risk, but is given by an individual who does not have sufficient expertise to understand such a technical concept.

Use of Investment Companies Rankings in Retail Communication

FINRA Rule 2212 sets forth the requirements that companies must follow to be allowed to include rankings of investment companies with retail communications. These guidelines are important to allow retail investors to have an understanding of the context of the ranking in terms of the characteristics on which the rankings are based and the funds against which the investment company is being compared. The rankings used in retail communications must be created and published by "Ranking Entities," which are defined as "any entity that provides general information about investment companies to the public, that is independent of the investment company and its affiliates, and whose services are not procured by the investment company or any of its affiliates to assign the investment company a ranking." Additionally, the headline must not state that the investment company is the best performer unless it is actually ranked first and must also disclose the name of the category, the number of investment companies in the category, the name of the Ranking Entity, the length of the period being evaluated, and the criteria on which the performance is based.

Example of a Violation

ABC Investment Company prepares an advertisement that states the following: "ABC Investment Company ranked first among large cap funds." This statement is in violation for FINRA Rule 2212 in a number of ways. While it properly defines the category, it does not state which ABC fund is being ranked. Additionally, for the statement to be in compliance, the ABC fund must actually be ranked first among whatever performance criteria was evaluated. The statement fails to disclose the evaluation criteria or the time period over which it was evaluated. Finally, the statement fails to disclose the Ranking Entity, if one was involved, and also fails to include the necessary disclosures relating to the use of past performance to assess future return expectations.

Requirements for the Use of Bond Mutual Fund Volatility Ratings

FINRA Rule 2213 provides guidelines for the use of Bond Mutual Fund Volatility Ratings. Since there are no clearly defined procedures by which these volatility measures are calculated, a number of important procedures must be followed and disclosures included. Any use of a bond mutual fund volatility rating must be accompanied by a prospectus and must also distinguish between volatility and risk and include supplemental sales literature reflecting the most recent available rating.

The rating must also be based on criteria and methodology that rely exclusively on objective and quantifiable factors and the rating itself must be clear, concise, and understandable. Finally, the entity that issued the rating must make additional supplemental disclosures and information available to participants upon request. Disclosures accompanying the volatility rating must include the name of the entity that prepared the rating, the most current rate date and an explanation of any change from the previous rating, and a narrative description of the criteria and methodology used in the rating.

Example of a Violation

ABC Company posts an advertisement on an online investing site stating that "XYZ Fund is the least risky large-cap fund available in the market based on the volatility ratings provided by DEF Investment Research in 2015." This statement is a clear violation of FINRA Rule 2213. First, Rule 2213 clearly states that a volatility rating cannot be used to describe volatility as risk. Additionally, the volatility rating cited in the advertisement is out of date and not the most recent volatility rating available. Such a statement would be misleading to potential investors. Finally, the advertisement does not include any of the required disclosure as to the methodology or criteria evaluated to produce the rating, and the rating itself is not clear and concise. It is a ranking instead of a volatility rating.

Requirements for the Use of Investment Analysis Tools

FINRA Rule 2214 provides guidance for the use of investment analysis tools, which are defined to be "an interactive technological tool that produces simulations and statistical analyses that present the likelihood of various investment outcomes..., thereby serving as an additional resource to investors in the evaluation of the potential risks and returns of investment choices." In order for a member to provide an investment analysis tool, the tool or generated report must include a description of the criteria, methodology, limitations, and assumptions, an explanation that results will vary with each use and over time, a description of the universe of investments considered in the analysis, and the following disclosure: "IMPORTANT: The projections or other information generated by [name of investment analysis tool] regarding the likelihood of various investment outcomes are hypothetical in nature, do not reflect actual investment results and are not guarantees of future results." The member must also provide FINRA's Advertising Regulation Department access to the tool and provide access to any written reports or retail communications concerning the tool within 10 days of first use.

Example of a Violation

ABC Company has generated a new investment analysis tool that allows investors to back-test a variety of investment styles and approaches over a period of time back to January 1, 2000. ABC Company has provided access to the tool to FINRA's Advertising Regulation Department and has included a disclosure that the tool is limited in its historical data and data prior to 2000 could significantly alter the results of the back-testing. While ABC Company has provided disclosure about the limitations of data, it has not included disclosure about the universe of investments that the model will consider, the assumptions made by the model, or the criteria the model uses to select investments for a given strategy. Additionally, ABC Company has failed to provide FINRA with copies of any reports or retail communications relating to this new tool. Finally, ABC Company failed to include the following disclosure, which must accompany the use of an investment analysis tool: "IMPORTANT: The projections or other information generated by [name of investment analysis tool] regarding the likelihood of various investment outcomes are hypothetical in nature, do not reflect actual investment results and are not guarantees of future results."

Communications with the Public About Variable Life Insurance and Variable Annuities

In addition to the guidelines set forth in NASD Rule 2210 with respect to communications with the public, additional guidelines are provided when the product under consideration is a variable life insurance contract or variable annuity. Additional considerations must be noted, including product identification, liquidity, and claims about guarantees. These additional considerations are required because of the difference in nature between these products and typical investment company products. Some specific additional considerations need to be considered as well, including presentation of fund performance prior to inclusion in the variable product, product comparisons, the use of rankings, descriptions of insurance and investment features of variable life insurance, and hypothetical illustrations of rates of return in variable life insurance sales literature. This last item is of particular importance because of the correlation between the investment performance of the funds within the variable product and the expenses and performance of the product.

Example of a Violation

ABC Insurance Company is offering a new variable life insurance product to the marketplace and follows all of the requirements for advertising for a standard investment company product. However, variable insurance products have some additional disclosure requirements. For instance, the advertisement must make it clear that there are significant liquidity constraints and tax implications, especially in the early years, for a variable life insurance product compared to a traditional investment. Additionally, ABC must be very clear about which features of the contract are subject to guarantees and ensure that the investor knows that the underlying fund performance is not guaranteed. The description of past performance of the funds offered within the variable insurance product must only date back to the inclusion of the fund within the insurance product, which may lead to a limited performance history for the fund in the early years of the product offering. Finally, ABC must be extremely careful about the use of comparisons or rankings to other types of investment products, as variable insurance products can have unique features that make them difficult to compare to traditional investment products.

Telemarketing

FINRA Rule 3230, which sets forth guidance on telemarketing activities, states that no member or person associated with a member shall initiate any outbound telephone call to:

- Any person's residence before 8 a.m. or after 9 p.m., unless:
  - The member has an established business relationship with the person,
  - The member has received that person's prior express invitation or permission
  - The person called is a broker or dealer.
- Any person that previously has stated that he or she does not wish to receive an outbound telephone call made by or on behalf of the member
- Any person who has registered his or her telephone number on the Federal Trade Commission's national do-not-call registry

Example of a Violation

John Smith, a registered person associated with member firm ABC Company, works from New York City and calls a prospective client at 9 a.m. Eastern Time. The prospective client lives in California. Mr. Smith has violated FINRA Rule 3230 because he has reached out to this client prior to 8 a.m. local time at the called party's location. There are only three circumstances under which Mr. Smith's actions would not be a violation of the rule. First, it would not be a violation if he had an established business relationship with the prospective client. It would also not be a violation if Mr. Smith had received express invitation or permission to call outside of the approved hours. Finally, if the prospective client is a broker or dealer, then Mr. Smith would not be in violation of the rule. It is important for registered persons to remember that the time-of-day restriction (between 8 a.m. and 9 p.m.) applies to the time at the location of the called party.

Prohibitions Relating to Interstate Commerce and the Mails

Section 5 of the Securities Exchange Act of 1933 sets forth several rules and prohibitions with respect to the use of interstate commerce and the mail service in selling securities. Specifically, the act prohibits the use of interstate commerce or the mail system to sell any security that does not have a registration statement in place. It also prohibits the sale of a security or the delivery of a prospectus unless the prospectus of such security conforms to Section 10 of the Securities Exchange Act of 1933. Finally, securities cannot be offered for sale if the registration statement is the subject of a refusal order or a stop order prior to the registration date. These requirements do not apply in the case of emerging companies that are in discussions with qualified institutional investors or accredited investors.

Preceded by a Prospectus

Rule 153a of the Code of Federal Regulations defines the term "preceded by a prospectus" as provided in section 5(b)(2) of the Securities Act of 1933 to mean satisfying the following conditions:

- Securities of the same class as the securities that are the subject of the transaction are trading on that national securities exchange or facility thereof, trading facility of a national securities association, or alternative trading system.
- The registration statement relating to the offering is effective and is not the subject of any pending proceeding or examination under section 8(d) or 8(c) of the Act
- Neither the issuer, nor any underwriter or participating dealer, is the subject of a pending proceeding under section 8A of the Act in connection with the offering
- The issuer has filed or will file with the Commission a prospectus that satisfies the requirements of section 10(a) of the Act.

Trading Facility and Alternative Trading System

Rule 153a of the Code of Federal Regulations defines the term "trading facility" as a "trading facility sponsored and governed by the rules of a registered securities association or national securities exchange." Additionally, the rule defines "alternative trading system" as "an alternative trading system as defined in Rule 300(a) of Regulation ATS under the Securities Exchange Act of 1934 registered with the Commission pursuant to Rule 301 of Regulation ATS under the Securities Exchange Act of 1934." The definition of alternative trading system under Rule 300(a) means "any organization, association, person, group of persons or system that constitutes, maintains or provides a market place of facilities for bringing together purchasers and sellers of securities or for otherwise performing with respect to securities the functions commonly performed by a stock exchange within the meaning of Section 240.3b-16 of this chapter; and that does not (i) set rules governing the conduct of subscribers other than the conduct of such subscribers' trading on such organization, association, person, group of persons or system; or (ii) discipline subscribers other than by exclusion from trading."

Regulation of the Use of Manipulative and Deceptive Devices

Section 10 of the Securities Exchange Act of 1934, and specifically Rule 10b-5, state that it shall be unlawful for any person, directly or indirectly, by the use of any means or instrumentality of interstate commerce, or of the mails or of any facility of a national securities exchange,

- To employ any device, scheme, or artifice to defraud
- To make any untrue statement of a material fact or to omit to state a material fact necessary in order to make the statements made, in the light of the circumstances under which they were made, not misleading
- To engage in any act, practice, or course of business that operates or would operate as a fraud or deceit upon any person.

In connection with the purchase or sale of any security, such activities may include insider trading or omissions or misstatements of material facts.

Filing Timing and Acceptance

Pursuant to Section 10 of the Securities Act of 1933, the prospectus must be submitted along with the registration statement for a security, but is not deemed to be part of that registration statement. Upon submission, the registration statement of the security is effective on the twentieth day after filing, or earlier if approved by the Commission. Also contained in Section 10 of the 1933 Act is language regarding the timing requirements for information contained in the prospectus, which states that "when a prospectus is used more than nine months after the effective date of the registration statement, the information continued therein shall be as of a date not more than sixteen months prior to such use." This is to help ensure that investors are being provided with current and relevant information that can be used in their investment decision-making process.

Registration Requirements for Brokers or Dealers

Section 15 of the Securities Exchange Act of 1934 prohibits any use of the national securities exchanges, mails, or interstate commerce to transact or solicit transactions in securities without being registered in accordance with the provisions of the section. Brokers or dealers must furnish a great deal of information on an application to the Commission, and the Commission will then determine whether or not to grant registration to the broker or dealer. Within the first six months following registration, the Commission will inspect the broker or dealer to ensure it is operating in conformity with all applicable rules and regulations. Under Section 14 of the Securities Exchange Act of 1934, the Commission also has the power to censure, limit, suspend, or revoke the registration of a broker or dealer for certain specified actions or violations.

Section 15 of the Securities Exchange Act of 1934 sets forth specific actions that may result in the censure, limitation, suspension, or revocation of the registration of a broker or dealer. The broker or dealer will have the opportunity to appeal such action, but may come under scrutiny for any of the following actions, among others:

- Willfully and knowingly making misleading or false statements with respect to material facts in applications for registration or any other reports filed with the Commission
- A conviction within 10 years preceding the application involving security transactions, perjury, bribery, burglary, larceny, theft, embezzlement, fraud, or substantially similar activities
- Having been permanently or temporarily enjoined by order, judgment, or decree of any court from acting as an investment adviser, underwriter, broker, dealer, or similar roles
- Willfully violating, or aiding, abetting, counseling or inducing another in violating, the Securities Act of 1933, the Investment Advisers Act of 1940, the Investment Company Act of 1940, or the Commodity Exchange Act

Manipulative, Deceptive or Fraudulent Devices or Contrivances

Rule 15(c)(1)-2 of the Code of Federal Regulations defines the term manipulative, deceptive, or other fraudulent device or contrivance as including "any act, practice, or course of business which operates or would operate as a fraud or deceit upon any person." The Rule further goes on to define the term "to include any untrue statement of a material fact and any omission to state a material fact necessary in order to make the statements made, in light of the circumstances under which they are made, not misleading, which statement or omission is made with knowledge or reasonable grounds to believe that it is untrue or misleading." The prohibition of using such manipulative, deceptive, or other fraudulent devices seeks to protect investors from the actions of brokers and dealers who largely control the flow of information and knowledge during a security transaction.

Section 15(c)(1) of the Securities Exchange Act of 1934 states that "No broker or dealer shall make use of the mails or any means or instrumentality of interstate commerce to effect any transaction in, or to induce or attempt to induce the purchase or sale of, any security (other than commercial paper, bankers' acceptances or commercial bills), or any security-based swap agreement, by means of any manipulative, deceptive, or other fraudulent device or contrivance." This relatively broad provision prohibits the use of any dishonest means by a broker or dealer to transact in any securities. While certain instruments are excluded from this provision, such as commercial paper, bankers' acceptances, and commercial bills, it does not mean that manipulative, deceptive, or fraudulent practices are encouraged in the sale of those products; it just means that those are not covered under this specific section of the Act.

Rule 15(c)(1)-7 of the Code of Federal Regulations further clarifies the application of the definition of manipulative, deceptive, or other fraudulent devices or contrivances with respect to discretionary accounts. Within a discretionary account, the broker or dealer is vested with discretionary power to affect purchase or sale transactions, and it is considered to be a manipulative, deceptive, or fraudulent practice if the transactions affected by the broker or dealer are excessive in size or frequency in light of the characteristics of the account in question. In order to be in compliance, brokers and dealers must also ensure that after each discretionary transaction in these accounts, they record such transaction, including the name of the customer, the name, amount, and price of the security, and the date and time of the transaction.

Customer and the Completion of the Transaction

Rule 15(c)(1) of the Code of Federal Regulations defines "customer" to "not include a broker or dealer or a municipal securities dealer; provided, however, that the term 'customer' shall include a municipal securities dealer (other than a broker or dealer) with respect to transactions in securities other than municipal securities." Under the Rule, there are variations of the definition for "completion of the transaction" depending on the parties involved. The most common definition involves a customer who purchases a security through or from a broker, dealer, or municipal securities dealer. In that case, the completion of the transaction occurs at "the time when such customer pays the broker, dealer or municipal securities dealer any part of the purchase price, or, if payment is effected by a bookkeeping entry, the time when such bookkeeping entry is made by the broker, dealer or municipal securities dealer for any part of the purchase price."

Misrepresentation by Brokers, Dealers, or Municipal Securities Dealers

Rule 15(c)(1)-3 of the Code of Federal Regulations describes more specifically what is meant, and what is not meant, by the registration of a broker or dealer. It is considered a misrepresentation and the use of a manipulative, deceptive, or other fraudulent device or contrivance to represent that registration, or the failure of the Commission to suspend or revoke such registration, indicates that the Commission has passed favorable judgment on the financial standing, business, or conduct of the broker or dealer, or has approved the merits or a particular security or transaction. The registration only indicates that the broker or dealer has met all requirements to be registered and is able to transact in securities in accordance with the rules and regulations applicable to registered brokers and dealers.

Requirements for the Delivery of a Prospectus, Preliminary Prospectus, and Final Prospectus

In order to not be considered a deceptive act or practice, a broker or dealer must meet the following requirements in connection with the distribution of securities:

- The broker or dealer must deliver a copy of the preliminary prospectus to any person who is expected to receive a confirmation of sale at least 48 hours prior to the sending of such confirmation
- A broker or dealer must take reasonable steps to meet requests for a preliminary prospectus between the filing date and a reasonable time prior to the effective date of the registration statement

- A broker or dealer must take reasonable steps to meet requests for a final prospectus between the effective date of the registration statement and the later of either the termination of such distribution or the applicable 40- or 90-day period
- A broker or dealer must make reasonable steps to make a copy of the preliminary and final prospectuses available to each associated person who is expected to solicit customers' orders
- If the broker or dealer is the managing underwriter, he must make sure that any broker or dealer participating in the distribution has reasonable quantities of the preliminary and final prospectuses.

Delivery of the Prospectus to an Associated Person vs. Other Broker-Dealers

Under Rule 15(c)(2)-8 of the Code of Federal Regulations, there is a delineation between the provision of prospectuses depending on whether the receiving party is an associated person or other brokers or dealers involved in the distribution of the offering. With the preliminary prospectus, the broker or dealer must provide each associated person a single copy of the preliminary prospectus for the security for which he will be soliciting orders prior to the solicitation of any orders. With brokers or dealers involved in the distribution of the security, the broker or dealer must furnish a reasonable quantity of the preliminary prospectus upon request of the broker or dealer. A similar process holds true for the final prospectus. The broker or dealer must provide a copy of the final prospectus to each associated person who is expected to solicit orders prior to the solicitation of any orders. With a broker or dealer acting as a managing underwriter, a reasonable number of copies of the final prospectus must be made available to the distributing brokers and dealers upon request.

Deceptive or Misleading Name

Section 35 of the Investment Company Act of 1940 states the following: "It shall be unlawful for any person, issuing or selling any security of which a registered investment company is the issuer, to represent or imply in any manner whatsoever that such security or company – (A) has been guaranteed, sponsored, recommended, or approved by the United States, or any agency, instrumentality, or officer of the United States, (B) has been insured by the Federal Deposit Insurance Corporation, or (C) is guaranteed by or is otherwise an obligation of any bank or insured depository institution." The decision as to whether or not a name is misleading is ultimately made by the Commission.

Misrepresentation of SEC or NASD Review

Section 35(b) of the Investment Company Act of 1940 states that "It shall be unlawful for any person registered under any section of this title to represent or imply in any manner whatsoever that such person has been sponsored, recommended, or approved, or that his abilities or qualifications have in any respect been passed upon by the United States or any agency or officer thereof." Member firms and brokers and dealers are allowed to represent that they are registered with the Commission, but must be clear about what registration does and does not mean. Registration simply means that the member firm or broker or dealer has submitted all of the required paperwork and is not currently subject to a revocation or suspension of membership and is permitted to transact in securities as its licenses allow.

Example of a Misrepresentation of SEC Review

John Smith works for ABC Investment Company. Mr. Smith's business card reads as follows:

John Smith

Registered Principal

ABC Company, an SEC-approved company

Mr. Smith and ABC Company would be in violation of Section 35 under the Investment Company Act of 1940 for misrepresentation. Member firms and broker-dealers are prohibited from stating that registration with the Commission is an endorsement or recommendation of their firm or products. Rather, Mr. Smith and ABC should revise the last line of the business card to state "ABC Company, an SEC-registered investment company." It is perfectly allowable for members or associated persons to state that they are registered, but they must be careful not to insinuate that registration also means endorsement, recommendation, or approval.

FINRA Rule 2320

FINRA Rule 2320 – Variable Contracts of an Insurance Company – applies only to variable contracts, which are defined as "contracts providing for benefits or values which may vary according to the investment experience of any separate or segregated account or accounts maintained by an insurance company." Whole life insurance contracts, in which the cash value is determined based on the age and gender of the insured in relation to the face amount of the contract, would not be governed under this Rule. Along the same lines, a universal life insurance policy is credited with a rate declared by the insurance carrier. This rate is often determined based on the performance of the carrier's general account, the assets of which back the liability from the policy. Thus, there is no separate account created for these cash values and the policy is not subject to this Rule. A term life insurance policy requires the policyholder to pay a fixed premium for a given number of years to maintain a given level of insurance coverage. These policies have no cash value, and thus are not covered under this Rule. In a variable universal life insurance policy, the policyholder has the ability to invest the cash value of the policy in a number of separate accounts. This is the only type of insurance policy that is covered by Rule 2320.

Purchase Payment, Variable Contracts, Affiliated Member, Compensation (Cash and Non-Cash), and Offeror

As provided in FINRA Rule 2320 – Variable Contracts of an Insurance Company:

- The term "purchase payment" shall mean the consideration paid at the time of each purchase or installment for or under the variable contract.
- The term "variable contracts" shall mean contracts providing for benefits or values that may vary according to the investment experience of any separate or segregated account or accounts maintained by an insurance company.
- The term "affiliated member" shall mean a member that, directly or indirectly, controls, is controlled by, or is under common control with a non-member company.
- The term "cash compensation" shall mean any discount, concession, fee, service fee, commission, asset-based sales charge, loan, override, or cash employee benefit received in connection with the sale and distribution of variable contracts. "Non-cash compensation" is all other forms of compensation, including merchandise, gifts and prizes, travel expenses, and meals and lodging.
- The term "offeror" shall mean an insurance company, a separate account of an insurance company, an investment company that funds a separate account, any adviser to a separate account of an insurance company or an investment company that funds a separate account, a fund administrator, an underwriter, and any affiliated person of such entities.

When Receipt of Payment Is Deemed to Have Occurred

FINRA Rule 2320 deems that payment has been received at the time at which the purchase payment has been submitted and the insurance application has been submitted to and accepted by the insurance carrier. However, in certain instances, the payment may be considered to have been received when the payment is actually made, if both parties agree to the timing as such.

Because payment is not considered to have been received until the application has also been submitted and accepted, it is incumbent on the member to submit as promptly as possible to the issuer the completed application and the purchase payment, or at least a significant enough portion of the purchase payment to issue the policy.

Requirements That Must Be Met for a Member Who Is a Principal Underwriter to Sell Variable Insurance Contracts Through Another Broker-Dealer

FINRA Rule 2320 states that no member that is a principal underwriter is permitted to sell variable contracts through a different broker-dealer unless the following conditions are met:

- The broker-dealer through which the underwriter is selling must be a member.
- There must be an existing sales agreement in place between the underwriter and the broker-dealer.

The Rule also places restrictions on members relating to their participation in the offering or sale of variable contracts. Members are not allowed to participate unless the insurance company, upon receipt of a properly completed request for redemption in accordance with the terms of the contract, makes prompt payment for the amounts requested in accordance with the contract terms, prospectus, and Investment Company Act.

Sale of Variable Contracts to NASD Members and Persons Associated with Members

FINRA Rule 2320 provides for certain restrictions and limitations on the circumstances and types of compensation that can be paid to members and associated persons for the sale of variable contracts, as follows:

- No associated person of a member shall accept any compensation from anyone other than the member with which the person is associated.
- No member or person associated with a member shall accept any compensation from an offeror in the form of securities.
- Members are obligated to maintain records of all compensation received by the member or its associated persons, and such records shall include the names of the offerors, names of the associated persons, and amounts of cash and non-cash compensation.
- No member or associated person shall make or receive payments of non-cash compensation, unless it is under one of the following arrangements:
- Annual gifts per person do not exceed FINRA limits and are not based on achievement of sales targets
- An occasional meal, ticket, or comparable entertainment that is infrequent and not meant to raise any question of impropriety
- Reimbursement for training or education.

NASD Rule 2420

NASD Rule 2420 states that members shall deal with non-members at the same prices, fees, and terms and commissions as in their dealings with the general public. Additionally, the rule states that no member shall:

- In any transaction with any non-member broker or dealer, allow or grant to such non-member broker or dealer any selling concession, discount, or other allowance allowed by such member to a member of a registered securities association and not allowed to a member of the general public.
- Join with any non-member broker or dealer in any syndicate or group contemplating the distribution to the public of any issue of securities or any part thereof
- Sell any security to or buy any security from any non-member broker or dealer except at the same price at which at the time of such transaction such member would buy or sell such security, as the case may be, from or to a person who is a member of the general public not engaged in the investment banking or securities business.

Non-Member Broker or Dealer

For purposes of NASD Rule 2420, "non-member broker or dealer" is defined as any broker or dealer who makes use of the mails or of any means or instrumentality of interstate commerce to effect any transaction in, or to induce the purchase or sale of, any security, otherwise than on a national securities exchange, who is not a member of any securities association registered with the Commission pursuant to Section 15A of the Act, except a broker or dealer who deals exclusively in commercial paper, bankers' acceptances, or commercial bills. Interactions with this group, who are not subject to the same regulations and requirements as member firms, should be considered to be identical to interactions with the general public, meaning that no discounts, commissions, allowances, or special terms should be permitted.

Dealing with Non-Members

NASD Rule 2420 elaborates on the rules with respect to transactions with non-members for non-members in foreign countries. More specifically, those provisions will not apply to any non-member broker or dealer in a foreign country that is not eligible for membership in a registered securities association. However, for any transactions with a non-member in a foreign country where a selling concession, discount, or other allowance is allowed, the member will be required to have the foreign broker or dealer sign an agreement that the foreign non-member will confirm to the provisions of NASD Rule 2420 when making any sales to purchasers in the United States as a result of such transactions. Such an agreement ensures fair dealing for securities that can re-enter the marketplace within the United States and avoid arbitrage and misaligned incentives.

NASD Rule 2830

NASD Rule 2830 – Investment Company Securities – applies exclusively to the activities of members in connection with securities registered under the Investment Company Act of 1940. NASD Rule 2830 sets forth specific provisions with respect to sales charges for investment companies with and without asset-based sales charges and funds of funds. Additionally, the rule prohibits selling dividends and withholding orders. Purchasing for existing orders, purchases as a principal, repurchases from dealers, and sales charge refunds are also discussed. Finally, the rule provides important guidance regarding member compensation from selling the covered securities and important disclosures regarding "hidden" product features such as deferred sales charges that may be unique to these types of products.

Brokerage Commissions and Covered Account

NASD Rule 2830 provides for the regulation of securities of companies that are registered under the Investment Company Act of 1940. The Rule provides for the definition of a number of key terms, as follows:

- "Brokerage commission" shall not be limited to commissions on agency transactions but shall include underwriting discounts or concessions and fees paid to members in connection with tender offers.

- "Covered account" shall mean (A) any other investment company or other account managed by the investment adviser of such investment company, or (B) any other account from which brokerage commissions are received or expected as a result of the request or direction of any principal underwriter of such investment company or of any affiliated person of such investment company or of such underwriter, or of any affiliated person of an affiliated person of such investment company.

Prime Rate, Public Offering Price, Rights of Accumulation, Service Fees, Funds of Funds

"Prime rate" shall mean the most preferential interest rate on corporate loans at large US money center commercial banks.

"Public offering price" shall mean a public offering price as set forth in the prospectus of the issuing company.

"Rights of accumulation" shall mean a scale of reducing sales charges in which the sales charge applicable to the securities being purchased is based on the aggregate quantity of securities previously purchased or acquired and then owned plus the securities being purchased.

"Service fees" shall mean payments by an investment company for personal service and/or the maintenance of shareholder accounts.

A "fund of funds" is an investment company that acquires securities issued by any other investment company registered under the Investment Company Act of 1940 in excess of the amounts permitted under the Act.

Asset-Based Sales Charge, Deferred Sales Charge, and Front-End Sales Charge

An "asset-based sales charge" is a sales charge that is deducted from the net assets of an investment company and does not include a service fee. Asset-based sales charges may not exceed 0.75 percent.

A "deferred sales charge" is any amount properly chargeable to sales or promotional expenses that is paid by a shareholder after purchase but before or upon redemption.

A "front-end sales charge" is a sales charge that is included in the public offering price of the shares of an investment company.

For companies without an asset-based sales charge, the aggregate front-end and deferred sales charges may not exceed 8.5 percent of the offering price, subject to additional discounts for rights of accumulation, quantity discounts, and service fees.

For companies with an asset-based sales charge and that charge service fees, the maximum charge is 6.25 percent of the amount invested. If service fees are not charged, the maximum charge is 7.25 percent.

Selling Dividends, Withholding Orders, and a Refund of Sales Charges

"Selling dividends" means stating or implying that the purchase of a given security shortly before an ex-dividend date is advantageous to the purchaser, unless there are specific, clearly described tax advantages to the purchaser. This practice is prohibited under NASD Rule 2830.

"Withholding orders," in which a member withholds placing a customer's order for its own profit, is prohibited under the Rule.

A "refund of sales charges" is required if a security issued by an open-end management company is repurchased by the issuer or the issuer's underwriter or is tendered for redemption within seven business days of the original transaction. The broker or dealer must refund the full dealer concession to the underwriter and the underwriter must pay back to the issuer the underwriter's share of the sales charge.

Member Compensation for the Sale of Investment Company Securities

FINRA Rule 2830 provides for certain restrictions and limitations on the circumstances and types of compensation that can be paid to members and associated persons for the sale of investment company securities, as follows:

- No associated person of a member shall accept any compensation from anyone other than the member with which the person is associated.
- No member or person associated with a member shall accept any compensation from an offeror in the form of securities.
- Members are obligated to maintain records of all compensation received by the member or its associated persons and such records shall include the names of the offerors, names of the associated persons, and amounts of cash and non-cash compensation.
- No member shall accept any cash compensation from an offeror unless it is described in a current prospectus of the investment company.

Conditions Under Which Discounts Can Be Made to Dealers

NASD Rule 2830(c) states that "No member who is an underwriter of the securities of an investment company shall sell any such security to any dealer or broker at any price other than a public offering price unless such sale is in conformance with Rule 2420 and, if the security is issued by an open-end management company or by a unit investment trust which invests primarily in securities issued by other investment companies, unless a sales agreement is in effect between the parties as of the date of the transaction, which agreement shall set for the concessions to be received by the dealer or broker." It is important that the written sales agreement documenting the discount is documented in writing prior to the transaction to avoid changing characteristics of transactions and changing negotiations with each transaction, and also to limit more subversive dealings.

Execution of Investment Company Portfolio Transactions

NASD Rule 2830 sets forth seven prohibitions relating to the execution of investment company portfolio transactions, as follows. No member shall:

- Favor or disfavor the sale of any particular investment company on the basis of brokerage commissions received
- Sell shares of, or act as an underwriter for, an investment company if it is known that there is an agreement through which the company directs transactions to a broker or dealer in consideration for the promotion or sale of shares issued by the company
- Demand or require brokerage commissions as a condition to the sale of shares
- Offer or promise to another member brokerage commissions from any source as a condition to the sale or distribution of shares
- Circulate any information regarding the amount of brokerage commissions received by the member to other than management personnel
- With respect to activities as an underwriter, suggest, encourage, or sponsor any incentive campaign or special sales effort of another member
- Provide additional incentive compensation to salespeople based on expected brokerage commissions, recommend specific investment companies to sales personnel on the basis of brokerage commissions, share in the brokerage commissions with salespeople, or use sales of shares in an investment company as a factor in negotiating the amount of brokerage commissions to be paid on a transaction.

FINRA Rule 2090

FINRA Rule 2090 – Know Your Customer – requires advisors to use "reasonable diligence" when opening and servicing customer accounts. Part of this reasonable diligence is knowing the "essential facts" about every customer, including those required to (i) effectively service the account, (ii) act in accordance with special handling instructions for the account, (iii) understand the authority of each person acting on behalf of the account, and (iv) comply with applicable laws, regulations, and rules. The importance of this rule is in ensuring that each investor's account is handled in accordance with the investor's wishes and in accordance with all rules and laws. This provides peace of mind to the investor that his account is being maintained and serviced properly not only at the account opening, but throughout the entire length of the relationship that the investor maintains with that advisor.

Essential Facts

The four "essential facts" contemplated in FINRA Rule 2090 – Know Your Customer – are those required to (i) effectively service the customer's account, (ii) act in accordance with any special handling instructions for the account, (iii) understand the authority of each person acting on behalf of the customer, and (iv) comply with applicable laws, regulations, and rules. These essential facts are important because they help to provide peace of mind to investors that their accounts are being handled in accordance with their requests. Additionally, they can be assured that only those individuals with proper authority to act on behalf of their account will be allowed to do so and that the account will be operated in accordance with all of the applicable rules and regulations. This responsibility lies with the broker or advisor, who are the experts in these rules and regulations, and not with the individual investor, who likely is not familiar with these rules or does not have time to constantly monitor and ensure compliance.

FINRA Rule 2111

FINRA Rule 2111 – Suitability – states that an advisor must have a reasonable basis to believe that the investment(s) he is recommending is suitable for the investor based on the information collected during the due-diligence process, including age, other investments, financial objectives, tax status, investment experience, time horizon, liquidity needs, and risk tolerance. This reasonable basis for an investment recommendation is critically important in helping to protect investors from making investments that may not be suitable for their financial situation. Specifically, investors may often be lured into investments with potentially attractive returns, but with correspondingly great risks. While investments like these may be suitable for investors with significant other wealth and assets or experienced investors, this would not be a suitable recommendation for a new investor whose investment represents a significant portion of his personal assets. Additionally, this Rule puts much of the responsibility for determining a suitable investment onto the advisor, who must educate his client on the risks and potential benefits of each investment alternative under consideration.

The new FINRA Rule 2111 expands upon the previous NASD Rule 2310 by specifying the factors to be considered in developing the investment profile, including an investor's age, other investments, financial situation and needs, tax status, investment objectives, investment experience, investment time horizon, liquidity needs, risk tolerance, and any other information disclosed by the investor. This is an important expansion because the delineation of these factors provides more clarity for advisors on the most important factors that need to be considered for each investor to which they make a recommendation.

The new Rule 2111 also provides that, while the Rule applies to all recommended investment strategies and the term strategy is meant to be applied broadly, the Rule does not cover general educational materials that firms may produce, as FINRA believes this educational material to be important to creating an educated investing public. This educational material is exempt from the rule so long as it does not include any specific recommendations of particular securities.

The new factors added to FINRA Rule 2111 include an investor's age, investment experience, time horizon, liquidity needs, and risk tolerance.

An investor's age and time horizon are typically closely linked and both are important in determining suitability because a younger investor will typically have a longer time horizon than an older investor, and will thus be able to take more risk than an older investor with a shorter time horizon.

An investor's investment experience will help the advisor in determining whether a more complex investment may be appropriate. An investor with more experience is likely more familiar with investment analysis and more likely to understand complex risks, while a novice investor may require more education from the advisor prior to making any recommendations.

Liquidity needs are also important in determining a suitable recommendation in terms of both the timing and magnitude of the liquidity requirement. An investor with near-term liquidity needs or a larger liquidity need must ensure that any investments can be quickly converted to cash to meet current obligations. To minimize losses and optimize performance, these investments should typically be much less risky in nature because of their short time horizon.

Finally, an investor's risk tolerance must also be considered, as the advisor will want to ensure that the investor understands and is comfortable with the level of risk in his portfolio.

FINRA Rule 2150

Pursuant to FINRA Rule 2150, no member or associated person is permitted to guarantee a customer against losses in a securities transaction. The goal of this prohibition is to ensure that the member or associated person does not become a party to the transaction in a greater role, that of guarantor. The security being purchased, and all of its risks, are outlined in the security's prospectus and statement of additional information, and the member or associated person must not provide any additional incentives or guarantees to entice the customer to purchase the security. Not only would these additional incentives and guarantees entice investors to make unsuitable investments, but it is not likely that representatives could provide the financial backing to step in to provide the guarantee in case of losses.

Sharing in Accounts

As it relates to sharing in the profits and losses in a customer's account, FINRA Rule 2150 prohibits this unless:

- The associated person receives prior written authorization from both the member and the customer, and the associated person shares in the performance of the account in direct proportion to the contributions made to the account by that person
- The associated person is sharing in the account with immediate family and receives prior written approval from both the member and the customer.

One of the difficulties with sharing in accounts is the complexity of tracking gains and losses in direct proportion to contributions. It is important to identify the accounts where this must be tracked so that the member firm with which the registered representative is associated can track the proper, proportionate sharing of gains and losses.

Improper Use

FINRA Rule 2150 states that "No member or person associated with a member shall make improper use of a customer's securities or funds." However, the rule does not go on to further clarify what constitutes improper use. One such actual example of a violation of this rule occurred when a registered representative reached out to a number of his clients and had them write personal checks to him so that he could invest those funds in an asset management vehicle that he promised would provide great results. Beyond the illegality of the customers writing personal checks directly to him to invest, the asset management vehicle he was describing did not actually exist and the registered representative used the customers' funds for his own personal use. Such actions are clearly in violation of FINRA Rule 2150 and constitute an improper use of customers' funds.

Conditions Under Which It Is Permissible to Borrow from or Lend to Customers

As stated in FINRA Rule 3240, borrowing from or lending to customers is prohibited unless:

- The member maintains written procedures for such transactions
- The borrowing or lending arrangement is with a customer who is immediate family, or with a customer that is a financial institution in the business of providing credit or loans
- The customer is a registered person with the same member firm
- The lending arrangement is based on a personal relationship with the customer
- The lending arrangement is based on a business relationship outside of the broker-customer relationship.

These guidelines are meant to protect the broker-customer relationship and to ensure that all transactions between the two parties fit within the scope of appropriate transactions that are covered within the regulatory guidelines.

Fraudulent Interstate Transaction

As provided in Section 17 of the Securities Act of 1933, "It shall be unlawful for any person in the offer or sale of any securities (including security-based swaps) or any security-based swap agreement by the use of any means or instruments of transportation or communication in interstate commerce or by use of the mails, directly or indirectly –

- To employ any device, scheme, or artifice to defraud.
- To obtain money or property by means of any untrue statement of a material fact or any omission to state a material fact necessary in order to make the statements made, in light of the circumstances under which they were made, not misleading.
- To engage in any transaction, practice, or course of business which operates or would operate as a fraud or deceit upon the purchaser."

Example of a Situation That Would Constitute a Fraudulent Interstate Transaction

Section 17 of the Securities Act of 1933 defines what constitutes a fraudulent interstate transaction. One example of such a transaction is where a registered representative in California reaches out to a number of elderly prospective clients in Florida with promises of a "Guaranteed Income Fund" that will generate 10 percent per year in annual income while preserving principal. In actuality, the fund only generates 5 percent in income and 5 percent in capital gains, and the fund has a five-year lock-up period on amounts invested. This registered representative has violated Section 17 by "obtaining money or property by means of any untrue statement of a material fact or any omission to state a material fact necessary in order to make the statements made, in light of the circumstances under which they were made, not misleading."

No Approval Clause

Section 23 of the Securities Act of 1933, often referred to as the "no approval clause." is meant to indicate to investors that while the SEC is responsible for approving the registration of a security, it is in no way responsible for the truth and accuracy of the registration statement and does not warrant the security as being a good investment. The Act reads as follows, "Neither the fact that the registration statement for a security has been filed or is in effect nor the fact that a stop order is not in effect with respect thereto shall be deemed a finding by the Commission that registration statement is true and accurate on its face or that it does not contain an untrue statement of fact or omit to state a material fact, or be held to mean that the Commission has in any way passed upon the merits of, or given approval to, such security. It shall be unlawful to make, or cause to be made, to any prospective purchaser any representation contrary to the foregoing provisions of this section."

Example of a Situation That Would Constitute a Misrepresentation Under the No Approval Clause

Section 23 of the Securities Act of 1933, often referred to as the "no approval clause," is meant to indicate to investors that while the SEC is responsible for approving the registration of a security, it is in no way responsible for the truth and accuracy of the registration statement and does not warrant the security as being a good investment. As an example, ABC Company includes in an advertisement that its new XYZ Real Estate Fund is recommended by the SEC. While it may be true that the SEC has approved the registration of the fund, ABC Company is not permitted to state that the SEC has recommended or approved the merits of the fund or deemed it to be a good investment. Such a statement would be misleading to investors, and the legislation has been designed to protect investors from such deception.

Front Running

According to NASD IM-2110-3, a broker-dealer is prohibited from buying or selling a security or an option on a security while in possession of material, non-public information concerning an imminent block transaction in the security or option on the security. It is important to note that trades placed through automated execution systems would not be covered under this rule, as the member would have established the rules for that trade prior to knowledge of the new block order. The illegality of front running is meant to protect investors from members and associated persons who are privy to material, non-public information about upcoming block trades. The rule prevents members and associated persons from using information gathered about a large upcoming block trade to submit trades in advance of those trades to capitalize on the price movements that will result from the large block trade.

Selling Away

According to NASD Rule 3040, selling securities without processing the order through your firm and without your firm's permission or knowledge is a violation of FINRA rules. This Rule prohibiting selling away applies to all securities, which may even include leasing arrangements or promissory notes, depending on federal or state law. It is important for associated persons to get written approval of any outside business activities prior to engaging in those activities so that the firm can adequately perform its supervisory duties. The member firm is responsible for supervising all associated persons, even if the business in which they are involved is unrelated to the business of the member firm. Those transactions of the associated person must also be recorded on the member firm's books and records.

Giving Gifts Beyond the Allowable Limit

FINRA Rule 3220 – Influencing or Rewarding Employees of Others – prohibits members and persons associated with members from giving anything of value greater than $100 per individual per year to any person where such payment is in relation to the business of the employer of the recipient. The rule also applies to gratuities, including gifts. Recipients covered under this rule include any person, principal, proprietor, employee agent, or representative where the exchange is in relation to the business of that individual's employer. If this rule was violated, it may result in biased and inappropriate decisions being made with respect to business relationships and customers' funds and accounts.

Churning

Churning, which is covered under NASD IM-2310-2, is defined as "frequent trading, or trading that is not consistent with the financial goals and risk tolerance of your customer, in a discretionary account (or account over which you have de facto discretion)." One of the most important FINRA principles is the protection of customers' funds and accounts, and churning is a direct violation of the trust and responsibility given to members and associated persons. The most common reason for members to commit this violation is to generate additional commissions and create a false sense of transaction activity. Excessive transactions generate excessive charges, reducing customers' account values without generating any additional benefit for anyone other than the member.

Refunding Sales Charges

When investors purchase Class A shares of certain mutual funds, they may be able to qualify for breakpoint discounts. In order to qualify for these discounts, investors must either invest a certain amount into that fund (often at least $50,000), sign a letter of intent to invest a given amount over a certain period of time, or combine purchases with prior purchases or purchases of other funds from that same fund family under rights of accumulation. While each mutual fund family sets its own thresholds and criteria for receiving breakpoint discounts, FINRA requires that firms must track whether customers are eligible for these discounts and must provide refunds if it finds that customers are eligible for refunds of previously paid sales charges. Additionally, FINRA may require the firms to pay interest on backdated amounts if they are found to have been previously due to customers. It is important for the protection of customers that FINRA continues to monitor and regulate the payment of these refunds.

Breakpoint Sales

FINRA Rule 2342 states that "No member shall sell investment company shares in dollar amounts just below the point at which the sales charge is reduced on quantity transactions so as to share in the higher sales charges applicable on sales below the breakpoint." It is important to note that just because the amount of a sale occurred just below a breakpoint does not mean that a violation has definitely occurred. FINRA will examine each case on an individual basis given the facts and circumstances, and will evaluate whether the trade was executed in a way that was designed to meet diversification and investment goals. The member must also disclose to the customer any breakpoints that are available at amounts near to the amount being purchased.

Forgery

The illegal practice of forgery occurs when an associated person of a member signs a document that is meant to be signed by another individual or poses as another individual in order to enact a transaction without that person's authorization or knowledge. Take the following example – an associated person of a broker is opening a new account for a client who has been a long-time friend. The account opening documents require the signature of the new account holder. However, the associated person knows that the customer is busy at work and forges his signature onto the documents. Even though there was not a malicious intent behind the forgery, it is still an illegal practice and compromises the integrity of the processes and procedures designed to protect both the member and the customer.

Switching

The illegal practice of switching occurs when a member or associated person moves a customer from one mutual fund to another when there is no legitimate purpose for the transaction other than to generate additional commissions and transactional activity. From the customer's perspective, there is cost and risk in this practice, as the transaction will generate new sales charges, cause realization of taxable gains on the prior mutual fund's earnings, and risk future investment earnings if performance of the new fund lags the old fund. This practice is in direct conflict of fiduciary principles under which the member should be acting in the best interests of its clients and where its own profitability should be a secondary concern.

Commingling Funds

The illegal practice of commingling funds occurs when an associated person of a member firm places customers' checks or money into a personal bank account or business account, regardless of the size of the deposit or the length of time the funds are held in the account. There are several reasons for prohibiting this practice. First of all, the recordkeeping behind multiple customers' funds being commingled in a personal account that is not subject to the same scrutiny as a customer's account could lead to confusion and a misallocation of assets among customers. Second, allowing individuals to deposit customers' funds into their own accounts could quickly lead to a misuse of those funds for personal reasons as well as delays in implementing the investing of those funds for customers. It is important for members to have clearly stated rules and procedures for any handling of customers' funds to avoid such situations.

Using Nonpublic, Material Insider Information

At times, members and persons associated with members will come across information that is considered to be nonpublic and material. The use of such information to gain an advantage for yourself or your clients is considered highly illegal and is one of the most widely publicized financial crimes. Material information is that which could be reasonably expected to influence your investment decision, and nonpublic information is that which has not been widely disseminated through an announcement or press release. The use of nonpublic, material insider information provides an unfair advantage to certain investors within the community, and often to those who are intimately involved in the inner workings of the subject company. Additionally, using nonpublic, material information could lead to an increased vulnerability to being subject to bad tips and trading on rumors and "hot tips" rather than confirmed data and information directly from the company.

Selling Dividends

The practice of selling dividends occurs when a member or associated person makes a recommendation to purchase a security immediately before, or sell a security immediately following, the payment of a dividend by the fund or company. In justifying this illegal practice, the member would tell the customer that they should purchase the security immediately prior to the payment of the dividend so that they would receive a higher return than had they waited. However, this argument is fundamentally incorrect, as the stock price reacts immediately following the ex-dividend date and the discounted cash flow stream generated from the payment of dividends is constantly factored into the stock price. This is a trick utilized by dishonest members to capitalize on a lack of knowledge by certain clients and to entice them to buy sooner, or sell later, than they otherwise might have.

Guaranteeing Against Loss

Members and persons associated with members are prohibited from guaranteeing against loss in an account. FINRA and member firms have no way to monitor and determine whether individual members and their associated persons are financially capable of providing such a guarantee and do not want customers to be able to be influenced by certain customers and members who claim to make such guarantees. The only time that a guarantee may be communicated to customers is when the underlying security includes such a guarantee (i.e., US Treasuries). It must also be communicated that such a guarantee is backed by the company issuing the security and not the member or associated person. Avoiding guarantees made by members and associated persons protects both customers and members from dishonest and unfair sales practices.

Oversees Compliance and Business Processes of the Broker-Dealer and Its Offices

Minimum Initial and Subsequent Investment Amounts for Mutual Fund Accounts

An open-end investment company, or mutual fund, allows a wide range of investors access to a wide array of investment products and financial tools. Without such access, an investor who wanted to diversify his account across a range of diverse asset classes and styles would need to purchase each individual security. Additionally, each security could only be purchased in whole shares. Thus, the minimum amount of investable assets required to properly diversify a portfolio would be substantial. Thanks to open-end investment companies, which often maintain small minimum initial and subsequent deposits, an investor can pool his money along with that of other investors and achieve access to partial shares of a number of securities, thus achieving diversification with a much smaller initial investment. Additionally, funds of funds allow investors to pool their money in order to gain access to funds with larger minimum investment requirements, thus providing access to additional investment strategies and asset classes that would otherwise not be available to the average investor.

Distribution Options for Dividends and Capital Gains

Many open-end investment companies, or mutual funds, provide services to investors through which any dividend income and capital gains distributions can be automatically reinvested to purchase additional fractional shares of the fund. Without this service, those dividends and distributions would typically be held in a cash or money market fund and would miss out on the earnings of the fund. At the time when a dividend is paid or capital gains are distributed, the investor's base upon which earnings accrete is reduced, thereby reducing total earnings until those funds are reinvested. Thus, minimizing the time that those funds are "out of the market" will help an investor to maximize his total returns. Additionally, fund companies do not charge for this service because it is in their best interest as well to have the investor reinvest those funds back into the fund to not deplete the fund's capital base. However, any fund distributions, whether reinvested or received as cash, will be taxed in the same manner.

Individual and Joint Tenants with Rights of Survivorship

An individual registration ownership of mutual fund shares means that there is only one individual owner and beneficial recipient of the securities in the account. Only this individual may authorize transactions on behalf of the account. When the owner of the account dies, the owner's will dictates the distribution of the account's assets. If no will exists, state and federal laws dictating estate distribution and beneficiaries will dictate the distributions. The other most common form of ownership for mutual fund shares is joint tenants with rights of survivorship. In this instance, the account has two or more owners who all share equally in the gains and losses of the account. Upon the death of one account owner, that portion is redistributed equally among all remaining owners.

Tenants in Common

Tenants in common is another form of mutual fund account ownership (in addition to joint tenants with rights of survivorship); however, these two forms differ from each other in a number of key features. For instance, whereas the account is owned in equal proportions by each owner within the joint tenants with rights of survivorship, the account can be divided into specific ownership proportions under tenants in common. The ownership proportions will determine the allocation of income among owners. Another key difference between these two joint ownership structures relates to the treatment of the account upon the death of one of the account owners. Under joint tenants with rights of survivorship, that portion of the account attributable to the owner who died is equally shared among the remaining owners. Under tenants in common, the deceased owner's portion of the account is passed to whomever is named in the deceased's will as a beneficiary.

Trust Accounts

In addition to custodial accounts for minors, the rules for which are set forth under the Uniform Transfers/Gifts to Minors Act, minors may also have accounts that are governed under a trust account structure. While trusts may be more cumbersome to establish and expensive than custodial accounts, they can also provide for additional flexibility that is not provided for under the Act. For instance, under the Act, that irrevocable gift that is made to a minor's account becomes her property immediately upon reaching majority age. Since this age is still relatively young to receive such a large sum of money, many families will choose to utilize a trust structure that allows them to control the amount and timing of when funds can be withdrawn from the account. Additionally, certain restrictive clauses can be placed on the trust account so that the recipients will only receive the money if they meet certain objectives (such as graduating from college). The funds in the trust and the restrictions placed on the funds are managed by the selected trustee, who will charge a fee for these services.

Custodial Accounts

Because minors cannot enter into contracts and thus cannot open accounts in their own names, there are a number of rules surrounding the opening of custodial accounts as governed by the Uniform Transfers/Gifts to Minors Act. The essence of this type of account is that it allows for someone to make an irrevocable gift of money or securities to a minor. However, those funds will be put into an account that will have an adult acting as custodian until such time as the minor reaches legal age, which varies by state. The Act stipulates that there may be only one custodian and one minor per account, that the custodian must act in a fiduciary capacity on behalf of the account, and that the minor is responsible for the income taxes on the account. Often, this is seen as a significant tax advantage and a means to efficient tax management, as the minor will have a much lower marginal tax rate than the adult who made the gift to the account.

Transfer on Death (TOD) Accounts

One popular form of registration for securities or ownership structure for securities accounts is known as transfer on death (TOD). In most accounts, the securities or account will go into probate along with the account owner's estate upon that individual's death. However, with TOD accounts, the account owner is able to specify the individual(s) to whom the account or securities should be transferred upon his or her death. By registering the account or securities in this way, individuals can avoid probate and ensure that their intended beneficiaries receive the account or securities directly, without having to rely on the executor or administrator of the estate. Typically, the only action required by the recipient of the account or securities is to re-register the account or securities in his own name. The specific rules around TOD accounts depend on the state law by which the account is governed, but most states have adopted the Uniform TOD Security Registration Act.

Uniform Transfers/Gifts to Minors Act

The Uniform Transfers/Gifts to Minors Act stipulates the rules and regulations under which it is permissible for a donor to make gifts or transfer assets to a minor. The minor has no right to access or withdraw assets until he or she reaches the age of majority as determined by state law. Until that time, a custodian will manage the funds or property in the account. The custodian has the discretion to manage the assets in the best interests of the minor and to use any funds or property to support the minor as needed prior to the age of majority. However, the custodian has no right to use any of the funds or property for his or her own use or benefit. Additionally, any taxes generated from the funds or property in the account are not the responsibility of the custodian.

FINRA Rule 4511

FINRA Rule 4511 sets forth three general requirements for opening new customer accounts, as follows:

- Members shall make and preserve books and records as required under the FINRA rules, the Exchange Act, and the applicable Exchange Act rules.
- Members shall preserve for a period of at least six years those FINRA books and records for which there is no specified period under the FINRA rules or applicable Exchange Act rules.
- All books and records required to be made pursuant to the FINRA rules shall be preserved in a format and media that comply with SEA Rule 17a-4.

The purpose of these requirements is to ensure customer protection by enabling FINRA to look back and examine all records related to the opening of an account, to ensure that the applicable laws and rules were followed and that the required due diligence was collected and presented to the client.

FINRA Rule 4512

FINRA Rule 4512 requires that for each new account that is opened, the following information must be collected and kept in the account's records:

- Customer's name, address, and age
- The names and responsibilities of any persons associated with the account other than the customer
- Customer's signature, or the signature of an authorized representative in the case of an institutional customer
- The names of any persons authorized to act on the customer's behalf
- For accounts that are not institutional accounts, the member must also collect the customer's tax identification number or Social Security number, the occupation and name and address of the customer's employer, and whether the customer is an associated person of another member firm.

All of this information is collected in order to protect both the member and the customer and to verify the identity of the customer to prevent illegal activity and unauthorized transactions.

Institutional Account

Under FINRA Rule 4512, an institutional account is defined as the account of:

- A bank, savings and loan association, insurance company, or registered investment company.
- An investment adviser registered either with the SEC under Section 203 of the Investment Advisers Act or with a state securities commission (or any agency or office performing like functions).
- Any other person (whether a natural person, corporation, partnership, trust, or otherwise) with total assets of at least $50 million.

For these institutional accounts, or for purchases on securities on which no recommendation was made by the member, the member does not need to collect and retain the customer information relating to the customer's tax identification or Social Security number, occupation and name and address of employer, or status as an associated person with another member firm. Essentially, the only information that needs to be collected in these instances would be the appropriate names, responsibilities, authorizations, and signatures for anyone acting on behalf of the account.

Information That FINRA Requires Members to Obtain Prior to Opening a Customer's Account

FINRA Rule 4512 requires that member firms collect and maintain the following information with respect to customers' accounts: the customer's name and residence, whether or not the customer is of legal age, the name of any associated persons responsible for the account and the scope of their responsibilities, the signature of a partner, officer, or managing director approving the acceptance of the new account in accordance with their adopted procedures, and, if the customer is a corporation , the names of any persons authorized to transact business. For non-institutional accounts, members should also collect and maintain the customer's Social Security number or tax ID number, the occupation and name and address of the employer of the customer, and whether or not the customer is associated with another member firm. Finally, for discretionary accounts, the member must collect and retain the name, title, and signature of anyone authorized to exercise discretion over the account.

FINRA Rule 4514

Generally speaking, FINRA Rule 4514 prohibits a member or associated person from obtaining check drafts or other negotiable instruments from customers. However, in the case where the customer has provided express written authorization, this may be permitted. The written authorization may be included on the instrument itself or be provided separately. If provided separately, the member or associated person involved in the transaction must maintain a copy of the authorization for at least three years from the date on which the authorization expires. The same recordkeeping requirements do not apply if the authorization is provided directly on the negotiable instrument. As with the other FINRA rules related to the maintenance of records, this rule is meant to protect customers and ensure that a proper paper trail can be constructed to resolve any potential disputes between members or associated persons and their customers.

FINRA Rule 4515

FINRA Rule 4515 sets forth clear guidelines with respect to the approval and documentation required in order to change the name or designation of an account. In order for the change in name or designation to be executed, a qualified registered principal of the member must authorize the change. Additionally, it is incumbent upon that qualified registered principal to be informed of all facts relative to the change and to record his approval either on the order itself or on some other documentation to be included in the file. All of the facts surrounding the change must be documented in writing and maintained in accordance with the rules regarding time and accessibility set forth in SEA Rule 17a-4(b). This protection is important to investors because it ensures that each change has been reviewed by a registered principal, and also because it ensures that a written record of the facts of the case will be maintained.

Timing of a Trade Execution and Account Name Change

Under FINRA Rule 4515, there are specific guidelines in place relating to the timing of trade execution when changes have been made to the account name or designation. More specifically, Rule 4515 states that all required approval and documentation surrounding the change of an account name or designation must be completed prior to the execution of any trades. Thus, the rule is attempting to eliminate the possibility of trades being placed in error or trades being placed in which not all of the required approvals or documentation have been completed, which may result in a trade being placed without the proper authority or under the wrong account name. This safeguarding of customer accounts is an important protection to investors and provides clear guidelines for members and associated persons on the actions required of them when changes are made to an account.

Requirements for Documentation

Unlike many other areas of the FINRA rules, there is no explicit documentation required when it comes to the content of the suitability of investment recommendations. Instead, FINRA will examine a number of areas of a firm's operations to determine whether its associated persons are making suitable recommendations to customers. Additionally, the security involved, the complexity of the transaction, and the specific facts and circumstances of the situation will drive the level of documentation that is required to prove suitability. Other areas considered by FINRA will include the level of training for its associated persons, the consideration of all customer information and the thoroughness of the information gathered, the source records for determining suitability, and the internal records used to determine suitability for at least some customers.

NASD Rule 2510

NASD Rule 2510 sets forth the authorization requirements and considerations around discretionary accounts, which are one of the most highly scrutinized types of accounts because of the transfer of power from the account owner to another individual and the possibility that creates for unscrupulous behavior. Within that context, regulators closely monitor discretionary accounts to ensure that members and associated persons are not making "excessive transactions." Rule 2510 states that "no member shall effect with or for any customer's account in respect to which such member or his agent or employee is vested with any discretionary power any transactions of purchase or sale which are excessive in size or frequency in view of the financial resources and character of such account." The motivation for a member or associated person to create such activity in a client's account is the increased commission revenue and higher perceived transactional activity, which may have other financial incentives at the member firm.

Authorization Requirements for Discretionary Accounts

For any type of discretionary account, whether full or limited, NASD Rule 2510 states that the member or registered representative must receive prior written authorization and the member firm must accept the account in writing. Under full discretionary authorization, a member has the right to purchase and sell securities, view account information, and transfer or withdraw funds as needed within any accounts covered under that authorization. While the member has the discretion as to the activity that occurs, all transactions and activities must still be done in the best interests of the customer and in accordance with the purpose of the account and the investment policy statement, if applicable. A limited discretionary authorization allows the member to purchase and sell securities within the account(s) without preapproval, but restricts that member from withdrawing or transferring funds between accounts.

Review Process in Discretionary Accounts

NASD Rule 2510 provides for two points of oversight and review of discretionary accounts by the member or a partner, officer, or manager appointed by the member. First, the member or an appointed representative must accept, in writing, every new discretionary account that is opened with the member. This review process must ensure that all necessary authorizations have been secured, whether the intent is to serve in a full or limited discretionary capacity. Additionally, the member or an appointed representative must provide additional protection to customers with discretionary accounts by promptly approving all orders in discretionary accounts and frequently reviewing accounts to ensure transactions are consistent with the financial resources and character of the account, and that excessive transactions have not occurred.

Settlement Cycle

Broadly speaking, Rule 15c6-1 provides that settlement of all securities, other than exempted securities, government or municipal securities, commercial paper or bills, or bankers' acceptances) will occur no later than the next business day after the date of the contract unless all parties agree at the time of the transaction. Additional exceptions to this settlement timing include transactions involving limited partnership interests that are not listed on an exchange or priced through an automated quotation system, securities exempted by the SEC, and transactions in cash or securities priced after 4:30 p.m. ET on the date of the transaction and as part of a sale through an underwriter. As it relates to securities issued through an underwriter, all securities may be subject to an alternate settlement date if so specified in the contract or firm commitment.

FINRA Rule 11310

FINRA Rule 11310 stipulates that members must utilize a securities depository for the book-entry settlement of transactions in depository-eligible securities with other members or members of a national securities exchange or registered securities association. Additionally, transactions are required to be settled by book entry using a securities depository for delivery-versus-payment or receipt-versus-payment transactions. Within the rule, a securities depository is defined as "a securities depository registered as a clearing agency under Section 17A of the Exchange Act." Depository-eligible securities are those that are eligible for deposit at a securities depository and are eligible for book-entry transfer at the depository at the time of settlement of the transaction. FINRA Rule 11310 does not apply to transactions settled outside of the United States or transactions where the securities to be delivered are not on deposit at a securities depository.

Delivery Dates

Under FINRA Rule 11330, transactions for cash require delivery to be made at the office of the purchaser on the day of the transaction and regular way transactions require delivery to be made at the office of the purchaser on, but not before, the next business day following the date of the transaction (T+1). Seller's option transactions require delivery at the office of the purchase on the date the option expires, except that delivery may occur on any later date prior to the expiration of the option if the seller delivers, on any business day preceding the day of delivery, written notice of their intent to deliver the following day. Finally, in buyer's option transactions, delivery must be made at the office of the purchaser on the date the option expires. The form of payment for such transactions is covered under FINRA rule 11330 and states that the party making delivery has the right to require purchase money to be paid by certified check, cashier's check, bank draft, or cash.

Regulation T

Regulation T, which was issued by the Board of Governors of the Federal Reserve System under the Securities Exchange Act of 1934, regulates the extension of credit to customers by brokers and dealers, imposes initial margin requirements, and imposes payment rules on certain securities transactions. As it relates to the timing of payment for securities purchased, Section 220.8(b)(1) states that a creditor shall obtain full cash payment for customer purchases within one payment period of the date that (i) any nonexempted security was purchased, (ii) any when-issued security was made available by the issuer for delivery to purchasers, (iii) any when-distributed security was distributed under a published plan, or (iv) a security owned by the customer has matured or has been redeemed and a new refunding security of the same issuer has been purchased by the customer. A "payment period" is defined within the regulation as the number of business days in the standard securities settlement cycle in the United States, plus two business days.

Extension of Time and Frozen Accounts

Regulation T, which was issued by the Board of Governors of the Federal Reserve System under the Securities Exchange Act of 1934, regulates the extension of credit to customers by brokers and dealers, imposes initial margin requirements, and imposes payment rules on certain securities transactions. Under the regulation, "extension of time" relates to exceptions that are provided to the timing of the payment and/or delivery of securities. In order to be granted this exception, the account owner must submit an application and be believed to be acting in good faith by the creditor. These exceptions are important because they provide some discretion and flexibility to correct for potential delays that are outside the control of the customer or the creditor. The freezing of an account, or the 90-day freeze, shall occur when a nonexempted security in a customer's account is sold or delivered to another broker or dealer without having been previously paid for in full by the customer. The freeze refers to the fact that the customer will not, for a period of 90 days, be able to delay payment beyond the trade date.

Rules Determining Permissibility of Arranging for Loans by Others

Regulation T, which was issued by the Board of Governors of the Federal Reserve System under the Securities Exchange Act of 1934, regulates the extension of credit to customers by brokers and dealers, imposes initial margin requirements, and imposes payment rules on certain securities transactions. Under Section 220.3(g) of the Regulation, it is provided that a creditor may arrange for the extension or maintenance of credit to or for any customer by any person, provided the creditor does not willfully arrange credit that violates parts 221 or 224 of the chapter. Part 221 sets forth credit restrictions for lenders other than brokers and dealers that extend credit for buying or carrying margin stock. Part 224 requires that credit obtained either within or outside of the United States complies with Regulation T and Regulation U.

Difference in Provisions Between Retail and Wholesale Transactions

NASD Rule 2830(m) stipulates the timing requirements for the transmission of payments for investment company shares, either for members that engage in wholesale transactions and payments received from other members or for members that engage in direct retail transactions and payments received from customers. Members that engage in direct retail transactions must transmit payment by the later of either the third business day following receipt of a customer's order to purchase such shares or the end of one business day following receipt of a customer's payment for such shares. Members that are underwriters and engage in wholesale transactions must transmit payment by the end of two business days following receipt of such payments.

Information That a Broker or Dealer Is Required to Disclose to a Customer

Under Rule 10b-10 of the Securities Exchange Act of 1934, a broker or dealer is required, at or before the sale of a security, to disclose the following information:

- The date and time of the transaction (or that such information will be provided upon completion of the transaction)
- The identity, price, and number of shares or units of each security sold or purchased
- The name of the person from whom the security was purchased, or to whom it was sold, or the fact that this information will be provided upon the customer's written request
- The amount of any remuneration received by the broker from the transaction, unless governed by a previously written agreement with the customer on a basis other than transactional
- Whether the customer paid any odd-lot fees in connection with the transaction.

The disclosure requirements prior to or at the time of a transaction allow customers to monitor all trades being placed on their behalf. This is important not only so that customers can monitor the identity, amount, and price of securities that are bought and sold in their accounts, but also so that they can monitor the efficiency with which any orders are being executed. Additionally, the compensation disclosures provide important information to customers to ensure that their brokers and dealers are not receiving unfair compensation that could either sway the broker's or dealer's recommendations or reduce the performance of the customer's investments. Finally, several of the disclosure requirements and the statement about availability of additional information help to provide less sophisticated investors with guidance about the critical issues they need to be considering and monitoring. The timeliness in which this information is furnished, which is also governed by Rule 10b-10, is important in allowing the customer to make informed decisions about their account using timely, not outdated, information.

Customer Confirmations

FINRA Rule 2232 stipulates the timing and disclosure requirements for members to notify customers of transactional activity in their accounts. Specifically, the rule provides that members must provide written notification to the customer at or before the completion of a transaction. The notification must include the settlement date of the transaction and, if the security is a callable equity security, both the fact that the security is callable and that the customer may contact the member for additional information. This rule is important for the protection of members' customers to ensure that they are aware of all activity within their accounts and also, in the case of more complex securities such as callable equities, to remind customers that they can reach out to the member firm for additional information and guidance.

NASD Rule 2340

NASD Rule 2340 provides that members must provide customers with an account statement at least once each calendar quarter. Such statement must contain a description of securities positions, money balances, account activity since the last statement, and a notice that the customer should promptly report, in writing, any discrepancies to the member firm. There are exceptions under which members may provide statements less frequently than quarterly, including when the account is carried solely for the purpose of execution on a DVP/RVP basis, all transactions are done on a DVP/RVP basis, the account shows no security or money positions at the end of the quarter, the customer consents to the suspension of statements, and the member undertakes to provide any statements to the customer upon request and reinstate delivery of statements upon request.

Account Activity and General Securities Member

Under NASD Rule 2340 "account activity includes, but is not limited to, purchases, sales, interest credits or debits, charges or credits, dividend payments, transfer activity, securities receipts or deliveries, and/or journal entries relating to securities or funds in the possession or control of the member." A general securities member "refers to any member that conducts a general securities business and is required to calculate its net capital pursuant to the provisions of SEC Rule 15c3-1(a). Notwithstanding the foregoing definition, a member that does not carry customer accounts and does not hold customer funds or securities is exempt from the provisions of this section."

Direct Participation Program and DVP/RVP Account

Under NASD Rule 2340, a direct participation program, also known as a direct participation program security, "refers to the publicly issued equity securities of a direct participation program as defined in Rule 2810 (including limited liability companies), but does not include securities on deposit in a registered securities depository and settled regular way, securities listed on a national securities exchange, or any program registered as a commodity pool with the Commodities Futures Trading Commission." A DVP/RVP account is defined as "an arrangement whereby payment for securities purchased is made to the selling customer's agent and/or delivery of securities sold is made to the buying customer's agent in exchange for payment at time of settlement, usually in the form of cash."

Registration and Regulation of Brokers and Dealers

Section 15 of the Securities Exchange Act of 1934 makes it illegal to act as a broker or dealer without being registered with the Securities Exchange Commission and provides the process by which firms must complete such registration. The objective of these provisions is to protect investors and the public interest by ensuring that the firms acting as brokers and dealers meet certain minimum requirements and are subject to supervision by the Securities Exchange Commission. Within 45 days of the date on which the application for registration is filed, the Commission must either grant registration or institute proceedings to further determine whether registration should be denied. If the latter occurs, the Commission must grant a hearing to the applicant firm. The proceedings may not last more than 120 days following the date of first application for registration.

Possible Actions of a Broker or Dealer That Could Lead to a Limitation of Activity or Suspension

Section 15 of the Securities Exchange Act of 1934 specifies a number of actions that could result in the limitation of activity or suspension, including:

- Willfully making a false or misleading statement or omission with respect to material facts within any application for registration or required reporting to the Commission
- A conviction within the preceding 10 years of any felony or misdemeanor involving the purchase or sale of securities, taking of a false oath, making of a false report, bribery, perjury, burglary, or conspiracy to commit such offenses
- A conviction within the preceding 10 years of any felony or misdemeanor involving the conduct of the business of a broker, dealer investment adviser, bank, insurance company, fiduciary, transfer agent. or ratings organization
- A conviction within the preceding 10 years of any felony or misdemeanor involving the larceny, theft, robbery, extortion, forgery, counterfeiting, fraudulent concealment, embezzlement, fraudulent conversion, or misappropriation of funds or securities
- Willfully violating or aiding and abetting the violation of the Securities Act of 1933, Investment Advisers Act of 1940, Investment Company Act of 1940, or Commodity Exchange Act.

RULE 15C3

Rule 15c3-3 states that "A broker or dealer shall promptly obtain and shall thereafter maintain the physical possession or control of all fully-paid securities and excess margin securities carried by a broker or dealer for the account of customers." This rule is an important protection for customers of brokers and dealers because it provides the guidelines for the custody and safekeeping of their securities. A broker or dealer being in control of the securities, rather than maintaining physical possession, may include one or more certificates in the custody or control of a clearing corporation or custodian bank, securities carried for a customer's account in the name of the broker or dealer with another broker or dealer, or securities that are subject to the terms of a bona fide repurchase agreement.

Subsection (k) of Rule 15c3-3 specifies the circumstances under which a broker or dealer may be exempt from the requirements of the rule, including:

- Meeting all of the following requirements:
- Transactions as dealer are limited to redeemable securities of registered investment companies or participation in an insurance company separate account.
- Transaction as broker are limited to redeemable securities of registered investment companies or participation in an insurance company separate account, solicitation of share accounts for savings and loan associations, or sale of securities for a customer to obtain funds to immediately reinvest in securities of registered investment companies.
- Prompt transmission of all funds and delivery of all securities.
- A broker or dealer that carries no margin accounts, promptly transmits all funds and delivers all securities, does not hold funds for customers, and processes all customer transactions through bank accounts specifically noted to be for the benefit of the customer.
- An introducing broker or dealer that clears all customer transactions on a fully disclosed basis with a clearing broker or dealer, promptly transmits all funds and delivers all securities, and maintains the books and records required of a clearing broker or dealer.
- A broker or dealer may petition the Commission and must prove that it has adequate safeguards in place to protect customers' funds and securities.

AGGREGATE INDEBTEDNESS AND NET CAPITAL

Aggregate indebtedness is defined as "the total money liabilities of a broker or dealer arising in connection with any transaction whatsoever and includes, among other things, money borrowed, money payable against securities loaned and securities 'failed to receive,' the market value of securities borrowed to the extent to which no equivalent value is paid or credited (other than the market value of margin securities borrowed from customers in accordance with the provisions of Rule 15c3-3 and margin securities borrowed from non-customers), customers' and non-customers' free credit balances, credit balances in customers' and non-customers' accounts having short positions in securities, equities in customers' and non-customers' future commodities accounts and credit balances in customers' and non-customers' commodities accounts." Net capital is defined under Rule 15c3 as the net worth of a broker or dealer, with further adjustments as detailed under the rule.

Regulation S-P

Regulation S-P (Privacy of Consumer Financial Information) contains at its core three main purposes or functions:

- The Regulation requires financial institutions to notify its customers of its privacy practices.
- The Regulation prohibits financial institutions from disclosing nonpublic personal customer information to third parties, unless the institution has disclosed its practices to the customer and the customer has failed to opt out of such disclosure.
- The Regulation provides certain industry standards for financial institutions regarding privacy practices and disclosure of customer information.

Through the various components of Regulation S-P, customers of financial institutions are afforded additional protection from the distribution of their personal information, while financial institutions are provided with a "road map" to follow to ensure they are staying in compliance with the regulation.

Disclosure Limitations

Regulation S-P (Privacy of Consumer Financial Information) provides for a number of improvements to the required disclosure by financial institutions to their customers regarding the institutions' privacy practices and providing of personal customer information to third parties. For example, financial institutions regulated under Regulation S-P must provide disclosure to customers including the nonpublic personal data that is collected, how that data is used, and with whom it can be shared. Additionally, the financial institution must provide the opportunity for its customers to "opt out," which means they can choose to prohibit the financial institution from sharing this information with third parties. As technology has spread and become an ever-increasingly important component of the financial markets, so too has concern over privacy laws, identity theft, and the protection of personal information. This is an issue that will continue to play an important role in consumer protection in the years to come.

Exceptions

Regulation S-P (Privacy of Consumer Financial Information) provides for certain exceptions to the disclosure and privacy policies. A good working knowledge of these exceptions is important to avoid confusion or miscommunication around practices that might otherwise be considered violations of the Regulation. For instance, the Regulation provides that the initial privacy notice must be provided at the beginning of the customer relationship, which is defined to occur at the time of share purchases. However, this privacy delivery requirement may be delayed if:

- Providing the notice prior to the customer relationship would delay the customer's transaction and the customer agrees to receive the notice at a later date.
- A nonaffiliated broker or dealer creates the customer relationship with the fund without the fund's prior knowledge.

Additionally, there are exceptions to the ability of the customer to opt out of the sharing of personal nonpublic information, when the institution must share that information with a third party in order to effect transactions on behalf of the customer or when servicing a customer's products and accounts.

Records to Be Made by Certain Exchange Members, Brokers and Dealers

Rule 17a-3 stipulates the books and records that must be maintained by all members of national securities exchanges that transact directly with other members and all brokers or dealers transacting in securities, including but not limited to:

- Blotters containing itemized records of the purchase, sale, receipt, and delivery of all securities
- Ledgers of all assets and liabilities
- Ledgers of all cash and margin accounts of each customer
- Each brokerage order, both executed and unexecuted
- Each purchase and sale for the account of the member, broker, or dealer
- Copies and confirmations of all purchases and sales of securities
- Detailed information regarding each cash and margin account indicating the beneficial owner
- All puts, calls, spreads, straddles, and other options where the member, broker, or dealer has direct or indirect interest
- Proof of money balances of all ledger accounts
- Questionnaires providing certain pre-approved information on each associated person of a member, broker, or dealer.

This Rule provides a clearly stated listing of all of the books and records that must be maintained by firms to ensure an adequate audit trail and provide a source of documentation in the event of a conflict that needs to be resolved.

Records to Be Preserved by Certain Exchange Members, Brokers and Dealers

Rule 17a-4 builds on the bookkeeping requirements of Rule 17a-3 by specifying how long certain records must be maintained by members, brokers, and dealers. Such requirements include:

- Records that must be maintained for a period of at least three years, the first two in an easily accessible place, including:
    - Checkbooks, bank statements, cancelled checks, and cash reconciliations

- Bills receivable and payable, whether paid or not, relating to the member's business
- Originals of all communications received and copies of all communications sent relating to the business, including sales scripts
- Trial balances, financial statements, internal audit working papers, and computations of aggregate indebtedness and net capital
- Guarantees of accounts, powers of attorney, and papers granting discretionary authority over accounts
- All written agreements entered into by the member, broker, or dealer.
- Records relating to closed customer accounts must be maintained for at least six years following the closing of the account.

Reports to Be Made by Certain Brokers and Dealers

Rule 17a-5 stipulates the reports that must be filed, and the timing of the filings of such reports, for brokers and dealers. The reports provided under this Rule must be filed either monthly or quarterly, depending on the specific report. Additionally, the requirements for reporting differ depending on whether the broker or dealer carries customer accounts or clears transactions. Those brokers and dealers that clear transactions or carry customers' accounts must file Part II of Form X-17A-5, while brokers and dealers that engage in more limited business that does not include carrying customer accounts or clearing transactions must only file Part IIA of Form X-17A-5, which is more limited in scope. Reports are considered to be filed once they have been received at the Securities Exchange Commission's principal office in Washington, D.C., and at the regional office for the region in which the broker or dealer has its principal place of business.

Financial Recordkeeping and Reporting of Currency and Foreign Transactions

Under Rule 17a-8 of the Securities Exchange Act of 1934, brokers and dealers are required to comply with the reporting, recordkeeping, and record-retention requirements set forth by the Bank Secrecy Act, the goal of which is to prevent and detect money laundering and other illegal financial activities. One such requirement of the Bank Secrecy Act is that brokers and dealers must implement Customer Information Programs that are designed to verify the identity of their customers, collect and maintain information necessary to identify their customers, and determine whether customers appear on any government-published lists of known or suspected terrorist organizations. Additionally, brokers and dealers ought to follow the training programs for educating employees on how to identify suspicious activity in customers' accounts and how to report such suspicious behavior to the proper governmental authorities, such as through Suspicious Activity Reports (SARs).

Financial and Operational Reporting Requirements

SEC Rule 17a-11 stipulates that "every broker or dealer whose net capital declines below the minimum amount required...or is insolvent...must give notice of such deficiency that same day." The notice must also include the specific amounts of the broker or dealer's net capital requirement as well as its current level of net capital. The rule also stipulates that brokers or dealers must report within 24 hours if one of the following occurs:

- Aggregate indebtedness in excess of 1,200 percent of net capital
- Net capital less than 5 percent of aggregate debit items
- Total net capital less than 120 percent of the required minimum net capital
- The fourth or more occurrence of a back-testing exception during any 250-business-day period
- Total amount of money payable against all securities loaned or subject to a repurchase agreement, or the total contract value of all securities borrowed or subject to a reverse repurchase agreement, exceeds 2,500 percent of tentative net capital

Rule 17a-11 is important to specify and ensure the prompt reporting of any significant deterioration in the financial status of a broker or dealer.

Requirements for Reporting and Inquiry with Respect to Missing, Lost or Stolen Securities

Rule 17f-1 stipulates the reporting requirements when securities are stolen, lost, or missing. For securities that have been stolen when there is reason to believe criminal activity was involved, the reporting institution is obligated to report the activity to the Commission and to the Federal Bureau of Investigation within one business day of the discovery and contain the certificate numbers of the securities. For securities that are missing or lost, the reporting institution must report the lost or missing securities within one business day of discovery that the securities have been missing or lost for at least two business days. The prompt reporting of these misplaced or stolen securities provides more opportunity for them to be recovered successfully.

Fingerprinting of Securities Industry Personnel

In order to verify their identity and protect securities industry customers and member firms, every member of a national securities exchange, broker, dealer, registered transfer agent, and registered clearing agency must require each of its partners, directors, officers, and employees to be fingerprinted and submit those fingerprints to the United States Attorney General. Certain exemptions are provided from this requirement, including partners, directors, officers, and employees of:

- Members of a national securities exchange, broker, dealer, or clearing agency who are not engaged in the sale of securities, do not have access to the handling or processing of securities, monies, or original books and records, and do not have direct supervisory responsibility for people with such access.
- Registered transfer agents who are not engaged in transfer agent functions or incidental activities.

- Registered brokers or dealers that are engaged exclusively in the sale of shares of registered open-end management investment companies, variable contracts, interests in limited partnerships, unit investment trusts, or real estate investment trusts; that maintain an updated Item 10 on Form BD relating to the disclosure of statutory obligations; that have insurance or bonding to indemnify it against losses to customers caused by the actions of its employees; and that are subject to the jurisdiction of a state insurance department with respect to the sale of variable contracts.
- Members of a national securities exchange, broker, dealer, registered transfer agent, or registered clearing agency who has tried on at least three occasions to obtain a set of fingerprints and submit them to the Attorney General but have had the fingerprints returned because they were illegible.

Disclosure of Financial Condition

FINRA Rule 2261 requires members to provide to their customers, upon request, information about the company's financial condition as disclosed in the most recent balance sheet, prepared in accordance with the member's usual practice or applicable laws and regulations. The "usual" preparation of the balance sheet is an important consideration so that the information provided is complete and not manipulated. The Rule also requires that any member that is party to an open transaction or has cash or securities on deposit with another member must furnish, upon request of the other member, this same financial information with the same preparation requirements. In both instances, the rule provides for paper delivery or electronic delivery, but a customer must consent to electronic delivery for this to be an acceptable method.

Capital Compliance

Under FINRA Rule 4110 – Capital Compliance – FINRA has the authority to prescribe greater net capital requirements or net worth requirements when necessary for the protection of investors or the public interest. Additionally, members must suspend all business operations when they are not in compliance with the net capital requirements, unless otherwise approved by FINRA. Finally, members may not withdraw equity capital for a period of at least one year from when it was contributed. Profits earned are not subject to this requirement. Payment of dividends, withdrawals of capital, or any similar distributions may not exceed 10 percent of a member firm's excess net capital in any rolling 35-calendar-day period.

Approval of Change in Exempt Status

NASD Rule 3140 only applies to members that are subject to SEC Rule 15c3-3, are not designated to another self-regulatory organization for financial responsibility, and are not subject to Section 402.2(c) of the Treasury Department rules. NASD Rule 3140 prohibits a member firm from substantially changing its method of doing business in such a way that the firm would be disqualified from exemption under Rule 15c3-3 or would change its exempt status under that Rule without first obtaining written approval from the NASD. Once the request for approval has been submitted to the NASD, it will consider the type of business of the member firm, the training, experience, and qualifications of associated persons, the member's financial and operational condition, and any other relevant information based on the facts and circumstances of that specific application.

Bank Secrecy Act

The Bank Secrecy Act, also known as the Currency and Foreign Transactions Reporting Act of 1970, serves to assist the United States government in uncovering and preventing illegal financial activities such as money laundering. Under the Act, financial institutions in the United States are required to report and maintain records for all cash transactions occurring in a single day in excess of $10,000. In addition, financial institutions must maintain records on their premises for a period of five years for any cash purchases of monetary or negotiable instruments between $3,000 and $10,000 in a single day. Finally, those financial institutions are also required to report any activity they feel to be suspicious or believe may be part of an attempt to conduct money laundering, tax evasion, fraud, or other illegal activities.

Under the Bank Secrecy Act, which is designed to prevent and detect money laundering and other illegal financial activities, financial institutions are required to collect certain data on the sender and recipient of funds for certain transactions. The information to be retained by the sender's financial institution includes:

- Name and address of the sender
- Amount that was sent
- Execution date of the transaction
- Payment instructions provided by sender
- Identity of recipient's financial institution.

The information for the recipient includes:

- Name and address of the recipient
- Account number of the recipient
- Any other specific identifiers of the recipient.

These requirements are important because they require the financial institutions to gather relevant data that may assist them in uncovering and preventing illegal financial activities. They also create a paper trail that can assist in future investigations, if necessary.

Anti-Money Laundering Compliance Program and the Customer Identification Program

Financial institutions and banks are required to implement Anti-Money Laundering Compliance Programs as part of the Bank Secrecy Act. A number of factors are considered in the development of each institution's compliance program, including the products and services it offers, customer demographics, and geographical locations, among others. Each institution must develop a comprehensive program that determines high-risk products or services, establishes monitoring and recordkeeping requirements for each line of business, and, finally, provides for a systematic approach to reporting and reviewing any suspicious activity.

FINRA Rule 3310 requires that each member firm develop and implement a written policy to detect and prevent money laundering. The program must be designed to comply with the Bank Secrecy Act and regulations from the Department of the Treasury, and must be approved by a member of senior management at the member. At a minimum, the policies must:

- Be reasonably expected to detect and result in the reporting of transactions required under 31 USC. 5318(g)
- Achieve compliance with the Bank Secrecy Act
- Provide for annual independent testing
- Designate and identify the individuals at the firm who are responsible for implementing and monitoring the program
- Provide ongoing training for all required personnel.

One component of an effective Anti-Money Laundering Compliance Program is an effective Customer Information Program, under which the financial institution gathers data to ensure that it knows the true identify of each of its customers. The information it collects on customers includes, at a minimum, the customer's name, date of birth, address, and identification number (such as a Social Security number). The institution must use some current form of identification of the customer to verify this information, such as a driver's license or passport. In the case of an institutional account, incorporation or trust documents may be used.

Securities Investor Protection Act

The Securities Investor Protection Act of 1970 was responsible for the creation of the Securities Investor Protection Corporation (SIPC), a nonprofit corporation charged with establishing the SIPC Fund to protect against the loss of cash and securities held by a customer at a financially troubled SIPC-member brokerage firm. SIPC protection is limited to $500,000, including a limit of $250,000 for cash. Money market funds are considered securities, not cash, in consideration of these limits. It is also important to distinguish that SIPC protection only covers the custody function of the broker-dealer and that your losses on the value of your securities would not be protected. Examples of types of funds not included under SIPC protection include currency, commodity or related futures contracts, or warrants or rights to purchase or sell currencies or commodities.

Membership, Exemptions, and Disclosure Requirements for Non-Members

Membership in the Securities Investor Protection Corporation shall include all persons registered as brokers or dealers, which the exception of (i) those whose principal business is conducted outside of the United States or (ii) persons whose business as a broker or dealer consists exclusively of either distribution of shares of registered open-end investment trusts or unit investment trusts, the sale of variable annuities, the business of insurance, or the rendering of investment advisory services to registered investment companies or insurance company separate accounts. Under the Securities Investor Protection Act, brokers or dealers who are excluded from membership in SIPC shall disclose their exclusion to customers living in the United States.

Process Whereby Customer Claims Are Filed

Under the Securities Investor Protection Act, once a trustee has been appointed, the trustee shall notify the public of the proceedings in one or more newspapers as approved by the court and also mailings to each customer on file within the books and records of the debtor member. Within six months following that time, the customer must file a written statement of claim, but not a formal proof of claim with the trustee, unless the person is associated with the debtor member firm or a beneficial owner of 5 percent or more of the voting stock. The SIPC Fund receives all amounts received by the SIPC, and all expenditures made by SIPC are made out of the Fund. The Fund was originally funded with a deposit of a minimum of $75 million and each member must deposit an initial assessment equal to 0.125% of gross revenues from the firm's securities business for the preceding calendar year. SIPC has the authority to determine ongoing assessments and may base those assessments on (i) gross revenues from securities business, (ii) composition of revenue from securities business, (iii) net capital, (iv) number of customers' accounts, or any of a number of other quantitative factors.

How to Overcome Test Anxiety

Just the thought of taking a test is enough to make most people a little nervous. A test is an important event that can have a long-term impact on your future, so it's important to take it seriously and it's natural to feel anxious about performing well. But just because anxiety is normal, that doesn't mean that it's helpful in test taking, or that you should simply accept it as part of your life. Anxiety can have a variety of effects. These effects can be mild, like making you feel slightly nervous, or severe, like blocking your ability to focus or remember even a simple detail.

If you experience test anxiety—whether severe or mild—it's important to know how to beat it. To discover this, first you need to understand what causes test anxiety.

Causes of Test Anxiety

While we often think of anxiety as an uncontrollable emotional state, it can actually be caused by simple, practical things. One of the most common causes of test anxiety is that a person does not feel adequately prepared for their test. This feeling can be the result of many different issues such as poor study habits or lack of organization, but the most common culprit is time management. Starting to study too late, failing to organize your study time to cover all of the material, or being distracted while you study will mean that you're not well prepared for the test. This may lead to cramming the night before, which will cause you to be physically and mentally exhausted for the test. Poor time management also contributes to feelings of stress, fear, and hopelessness as you realize you are not well prepared but don't know what to do about it.

Other times, test anxiety is not related to your preparation for the test but comes from unresolved fear. This may be a past failure on a test, or poor performance on tests in general. It may come from comparing yourself to others who seem to be performing better or from the stress of living up to expectations. Anxiety may be driven by fears of the future—how failure on this test would affect your educational and career goals. These fears are often completely irrational, but they can still negatively impact your test performance.

Elements of Test Anxiety

As mentioned earlier, test anxiety is considered to be an emotional state, but it has physical and mental components as well. Sometimes you may not even realize that you are suffering from test anxiety until you notice the physical symptoms. These can include trembling hands, rapid heartbeat, sweating, nausea, and tense muscles. Extreme anxiety may lead to fainting or vomiting. Obviously, any of these symptoms can have a negative impact on testing. It is important to recognize them as soon as they begin to occur so that you can address the problem before it damages your performance.

The mental components of test anxiety include trouble focusing and inability to remember learned information. During a test, your mind is on high alert, which can help you recall information and stay focused for an extended period of time. However, anxiety interferes with your mind's natural processes, causing you to blank out, even on the questions you know well. The strain of testing during anxiety makes it difficult to stay focused, especially on a test that may take several hours. Extreme anxiety can take a huge mental toll, making it difficult not only to recall test information but even to understand the test questions or pull your thoughts together.

Effects of Test Anxiety

Test anxiety is like a disease—if left untreated, it will get progressively worse. Anxiety leads to poor performance, and this reinforces the feelings of fear and failure, which in turn lead to poor performances on subsequent tests. It can grow from a mild nervousness to a crippling condition. If allowed to progress, test anxiety can have a big impact on your schooling, and consequently on your future.

Test anxiety can spread to other parts of your life. Anxiety on tests can become anxiety in any stressful situation, and blanking on a test can turn into panicking in a job situation. But fortunately, you don't have to let anxiety rule your testing and determine your grades. There are a number of relatively simple steps you can take to move past anxiety and function normally on a test and in the rest of life.

Physical Steps for Beating Test Anxiety

While test anxiety is a serious problem, the good news is that it can be overcome. It doesn't have to control your ability to think and remember information. While it may take time, you can begin taking steps today to beat anxiety.

Just as your first hint that you may be struggling with anxiety comes from the physical symptoms, the first step to treating it is also physical. Rest is crucial for having a clear, strong mind. If you are tired, it is much easier to give in to anxiety. But if you establish good sleep habits, your body and mind will be ready to perform optimally, without the strain of exhaustion. Additionally, sleeping well helps you to retain information better, so you're more likely to recall the answers when you see the test questions.

Getting good sleep means more than going to bed on time. It's important to allow your brain time to relax. Take study breaks from time to time so it doesn't get overworked, and don't study right before bed. Take time to rest your mind before trying to rest your body, or you may find it difficult to fall asleep.

Along with sleep, other aspects of physical health are important in preparing for a test. Good nutrition is vital for good brain function. Sugary foods and drinks may give a burst of energy but this burst is followed by a crash, both physically and emotionally. Instead, fuel your body with protein and vitamin-rich foods.

Also, drink plenty of water. Dehydration can lead to headaches and exhaustion, especially if your brain is already under stress from the rigors of the test. Particularly if your test is a long one, drink water during the breaks. And if possible, take an energy-boosting snack to eat between sections.

Along with sleep and diet, a third important part of physical health is exercise. Maintaining a steady workout schedule is helpful, but even taking 5-minute study breaks to walk can help get your blood pumping faster and clear your head. Exercise also releases endorphins, which contribute to a positive feeling and can help combat test anxiety.

When you nurture your physical health, you are also contributing to your mental health. If your body is healthy, your mind is much more likely to be healthy as well. So take time to rest, nourish your body with healthy food and water, and get moving as much as possible. Taking these physical steps will make you stronger and more able to take the mental steps necessary to overcome test anxiety.

Mental Steps for Beating Test Anxiety

Working on the mental side of test anxiety can be more challenging, but as with the physical side, there are clear steps you can take to overcome it. As mentioned earlier, test anxiety often stems from lack of preparation, so the obvious solution is to prepare for the test. Effective studying may be the most important weapon you have for beating test anxiety, but you can and should employ several other mental tools to combat fear.

First, boost your confidence by reminding yourself of past success—tests or projects that you aced. If you're putting as much effort into preparing for this test as you did for those, there's no reason you should expect to fail here. Work hard to prepare; then trust your preparation.

Second, surround yourself with encouraging people. It can be helpful to find a study group, but be sure that the people you're around will encourage a positive attitude. If you spend time with others who are anxious or cynical, this will only contribute to your own anxiety. Look for others who are motivated to study hard from a desire to succeed, not from a fear of failure.

Third, reward yourself. A test is physically and mentally tiring, even without anxiety, and it can be helpful to have something to look forward to. Plan an activity following the test, regardless of the outcome, such as going to a movie or getting ice cream.

When you are taking the test, if you find yourself beginning to feel anxious, remind yourself that you know the material. Visualize successfully completing the test. Then take a few deep, relaxing breaths and return to it. Work through the questions carefully but with confidence, knowing that you are capable of succeeding.

Developing a healthy mental approach to test taking will also aid in other areas of life. Test anxiety affects more than just the actual test—it can be damaging to your mental health and even contribute to depression. It's important to beat test anxiety before it becomes a problem for more than testing.

Study Strategy

Being prepared for the test is necessary to combat anxiety, but what does being prepared look like? You may study for hours on end and still not feel prepared. What you need is a strategy for test prep. The next few pages outline our recommended steps to help you plan out and conquer the challenge of preparation.

Step 1: Scope Out the Test

Learn everything you can about the format (multiple choice, essay, etc.) and what will be on the test. Gather any study materials, course outlines, or sample exams that may be available. Not only will this help you to prepare, but knowing what to expect can help to alleviate test anxiety.

Step 2: Map Out the Material

Look through the textbook or study guide and make note of how many chapters or sections it has. Then divide these over the time you have. For example, if a book has 15 chapters and you have five days to study, you need to cover three chapters each day. Even better, if you have the time, leave an extra day at the end for overall review after you have gone through the material in depth.

If time is limited, you may need to prioritize the material. Look through it and make note of which sections you think you already have a good grasp on, and which need review. While you are studying, skim quickly through the familiar sections and take more time on the challenging parts. Write out your plan so you don't get lost as you go. Having a written plan also helps you feel more in control of the study, so anxiety is less likely to arise from feeling overwhelmed at the amount to cover.

Step 3: Gather Your Tools

Decide what study method works best for you. Do you prefer to highlight in the book as you study and then go back over the highlighted portions? Or do you type out notes of the important information? Or is it helpful to make flashcards that you can carry with you? Assemble the pens, index cards, highlighters, post-it notes, and any other materials you may need so you won't be distracted by getting up to find things while you study.

If you're having a hard time retaining the information or organizing your notes, experiment with different methods. For example, try color-coding by subject with colored pens, highlighters, or post-it notes. If you learn better by hearing, try recording yourself reading your notes so you can listen while in the car, working out, or simply sitting at your desk. Ask a friend to quiz you from your flashcards, or try teaching someone the material to solidify it in your mind.

Step 4: Create Your Environment

It's important to avoid distractions while you study. This includes both the obvious distractions like visitors and the subtle distractions like an uncomfortable chair (or a too-comfortable couch that makes you want to fall asleep). Set up the best study environment possible: good lighting and a comfortable work area. If background music helps you focus, you may want to turn it on, but otherwise keep the room quiet. If you are using a computer to take notes, be sure you don't have any other windows open, especially applications like social media, games, or anything else that could distract you. Silence your phone and turn off notifications. Be sure to keep water close by so you stay hydrated while you study (but avoid unhealthy drinks and snacks).

Also, take into account the best time of day to study. Are you freshest first thing in the morning? Try to set aside some time then to work through the material. Is your mind clearer in the afternoon or evening? Schedule your study session then. Another method is to study at the same time of day that you will take the test, so that your brain gets used to working on the material at that time and will be ready to focus at test time.

Step 5: Study!

Once you have done all the study preparation, it's time to settle into the actual studying. Sit down, take a few moments to settle your mind so you can focus, and begin to follow your study plan. Don't give in to distractions or let yourself procrastinate. This is your time to prepare so you'll be ready to fearlessly approach the test. Make the most of the time and stay focused.

Of course, you don't want to burn out. If you study too long you may find that you're not retaining the information very well. Take regular study breaks. For example, taking five minutes out of every hour to walk briskly, breathing deeply and swinging your arms, can help your mind stay fresh.

As you get to the end of each chapter or section, it's a good idea to do a quick review. Remind yourself of what you learned and work on any difficult parts. When you feel that you've mastered the material, move on to the next part. At the end of your study session, briefly skim through your notes again.

But while review is helpful, cramming last minute is NOT. If at all possible, work ahead so that you won't need to fit all your study into the last day. Cramming overloads your brain with more information than it can process and retain, and your tired mind may struggle to recall even previously learned information when it is overwhelmed with last-minute study. Also, the urgent nature of cramming and the stress placed on your brain contribute to anxiety. You'll be more likely to go to the test feeling unprepared and having trouble thinking clearly.

So don't cram, and don't stay up late before the test, even just to review your notes at a leisurely pace. Your brain needs rest more than it needs to go over the information again. In fact, plan to finish your studies by noon or early afternoon the day before the test. Give your brain the rest of the day to relax or focus on other things, and get a good night's sleep. Then you will be fresh for the test and better able to recall what you've studied.

Step 6: Take a Practice Test

Many courses offer sample tests, either online or in the study materials. This is an excellent resource to check whether you have mastered the material, as well as to prepare for the test format and environment.

Check the test format ahead of time: the number of questions, the type (multiple choice, free response, etc.), and the time limit. Then create a plan for working through them. For example, if you have 30 minutes to take a 60-question test, your limit is 30 seconds per question. Spend less time on the questions you know well so that you can take more time on the difficult ones.

If you have time to take several practice tests, take the first one open book, with no time limit. Work through the questions at your own pace and make sure you fully understand them. Gradually work up to taking a test under test conditions: sit at a desk with all study materials put away and set a timer. Pace yourself to make sure you finish the test with time to spare and go back to check your answers if you have time.

After each test, check your answers. On the questions you missed, be sure you understand why you missed them. Did you misread the question (tests can use tricky wording)? Did you forget the information? Or was it something you hadn't learned? Go back and study any shaky areas that the practice tests reveal.

Taking these tests not only helps with your grade, but also aids in combating test anxiety. If you're already used to the test conditions, you're less likely to worry about it, and working through tests until you're scoring well gives you a confidence boost. Go through the practice tests until you feel comfortable, and then you can go into the test knowing that you're ready for it.

Test Tips

On test day, you should be confident, knowing that you've prepared well and are ready to answer the questions. But aside from preparation, there are several test day strategies you can employ to maximize your performance.

First, as stated before, get a good night's sleep the night before the test (and for several nights before that, if possible). Go into the test with a fresh, alert mind rather than staying up late to study.

Try not to change too much about your normal routine on the day of the test. It's important to eat a nutritious breakfast, but if you normally don't eat breakfast at all, consider eating just a protein bar. If you're a coffee drinker, go ahead and have your normal coffee. Just make sure you time it so that the caffeine doesn't wear off right in the middle of your test. Avoid sugary beverages, and drink enough water to stay hydrated but not so much that you need a restroom break 10 minutes into the test. If your test isn't first thing in the morning, consider going for a walk or doing a light workout before the test to get your blood flowing.

Allow yourself enough time to get ready, and leave for the test with plenty of time to spare so you won't have the anxiety of scrambling to arrive in time. Another reason to be early is to select a good seat. It's helpful to sit away from doors and windows, which can be distracting. Find a good seat, get out your supplies, and settle your mind before the test begins.

When the test begins, start by going over the instructions carefully, even if you already know what to expect. Make sure you avoid any careless mistakes by following the directions.

Then begin working through the questions, pacing yourself as you've practiced. If you're not sure on an answer, don't spend too much time on it, and don't let it shake your confidence. Either skip it and come back later, or eliminate as many wrong answers as possible and guess among the remaining ones. Don't dwell on these questions as you continue—put them out of your mind and focus on what lies ahead.

Be sure to read all of the answer choices, even if you're sure the first one is the right answer. Sometimes you'll find a better one if you keep reading. But don't second-guess yourself if you do immediately know the answer. Your gut instinct is usually right. Don't let test anxiety rob you of the information you know.

If you have time at the end of the test (and if the test format allows), go back and review your answers. Be cautious about changing any, since your first instinct tends to be correct, but make sure you didn't misread any of the questions or accidentally mark the wrong answer choice. Look over any you skipped and make an educated guess.

At the end, leave the test feeling confident. You've done your best, so don't waste time worrying about your performance or wishing you could change anything. Instead, celebrate the successful completion of this test. And finally, use this test to learn how to deal with anxiety even better next time.

Review Video: Test Anxiety
Visit mometrix.com/academy and enter code: 100340

Important Qualification

Not all anxiety is created equal. If your test anxiety is causing major issues in your life beyond the classroom or testing center, or if you are experiencing troubling physical symptoms related to your anxiety, it may be a sign of a serious physiological or psychological condition. If this sounds like your situation, we strongly encourage you to seek professional help.

Online Resources

Due to our efforts to try to keep this book to a manageable length, we've created a link that will give you access to all of your online resources:

mometrix.com/resources719/series26

It's Your Moment, Let's Celebrate It!

Share your story @mometrixtestpreparation